Wanderlust in Gay Asia

Exotic Encounters and Erotic Escapades

Wanderlust in Gay Asia

Exotic Encounters and Erotic Escapades

by Suzy Size
aka Hans Fritschi

Marshall Cavendish Editions

Design by Bernard Go Kwang Meng
Edited by Stephanie Yeo
Cover photo: Photolibrary

© 2011 Marshall Cavendish International (Asia) Private Limited

Published by Marshall Cavendish Editions
An imprint of Marshall Cavendish International
1 New Industrial Road, Singapore 536196

All rights reserved

No part of this publication may be reproduced, stored in a retrieval system or transmitted, in any form or by any means, electronic, mechanical, photocopying, recording or otherwise, without the prior permission of the copyright owner. Request for permission should be addressed to the Publisher, Marshall Cavendish International (Asia) Private Limited, 1 New Industrial Road, Singapore 536196. Tel: (65) 6213 9300, Fax: (65) 6285 4871. E-mail: te@sg.marshallcavendish.com

The publisher makes no representation or warranties with respect to the contents of this book, and specifically disclaims any implied warranties or merchantability or fitness for any particular purpose, and shall in no events be liable for any loss of profit or any other commercial damage, including but not limited to special, incidental, consequential, or other damages.

Other Marshall Cavendish Offices:
Marshall Cavendish International. PO Box 65829, London EC1P 1NY, UK • Marshall Cavendish Corporation. 99 White Plains Road, Tarrytown NY 10591-9001, USA • Marshall Cavendish Intxernational (Thailand) Co Ltd. 253 Asoke, 12th Flr, Sukhumvit 21 Road, Klongtoey Nua, Wattana, Bangkok 10110, Thailand • Marshall Cavendish (Malaysia) Sdn Bhd, Times Subang, Lot 46, Subang Hi-Tech Industrial Park, Batu Tiga, 40000 Shah Alam, Selangor Darul Ehsan, Malaysia.

Marshall Cavendish is a trademark of Times Publishing Limited

National Library Board, Singapore Cataloguing-in-Publication Data
Fritschi, Hans, 1957-
Wanderlust in gay Asia : exotic encounters and erotic escapades / by Hans Fritschi. - Singapore : Marshall Cavendish Editions, c2011.
p. cm.
ISBN : 978-981-4328-35-7 (pbk.)

1. Fritschi, Hans, 1957- - Travel - Asia. 2. Gay men - Travel - Asia.
3. Asia - Description and travel. I. Title.

HQ75.26
915.0086642 -- dc22   OCN689921169

Printed in Singapore by Fabulous Printers Pte Ltd

CONTENTS

6		Introduction
8	01	Call Boy (Thailand)
12	02	Wanderlust (Malaysia, Singapore, Indonesia, Cambodia, Vietnam)
88	03	Hugo (Thailand)
93	04	Of Superman and Less Superb Men (Macau, Hong Kong, Manila, Taipei)
121	05	Extras (Thailand)
124	06	In India, Nothing is What it Seems (India)
163	07	Boat Races (Thailand)
169	08	Big Fish in China (China, Laos)
206	09	Bobby (Thailand)
210	10	Golden Horn Istanbul (Turkey)
220	11	Gay Chiang Mai Revisited (Thailand)
225	12	Love Tragedies and Comedies (Sri Lanka)
240	13	A Night in Bangkok Still Makes a Hard Man Stumble (Thailand)
251	14	Battles (Thailand)
256		About the Author

INTRODUCTION

When my business partner and best friend Stefan Matter was diagnosed with cancer five years ago, he temporarily returned to our common home country Switzerland for proper treatment, including nasty chemotherapy. In addition to my editorial work in our publishing company, I had to take over the general management from him with no notice. This was a hard time with lots of work and many worries.

Stefan has since overcome his illness, but the event was a wake-up call: we all have to die one day. That was when we decided to sell the business, have some fun while we are still alive and stop working. Within a year we had sold everything and were free of any daily obligations.

But I am not the type for early retirement at 50. I was terribly unhappy just cooking or gardening or going to Jomtien beach to read each and every day. I had to re-invent myself.

When we had sold the print version of our gay magazine *Sticky Rice* (formerly *Thai Guys*), I kept the website *www.stickyrice.ws*, which had considerable traffic. I decided to turn this into a Gay Guide for Thailand. But soon I had visited everywhere in Thailand, listed the main places in our Pink Pages and described the scene. I then decided to expand my website into a Gay Guide for the whole of Asia. That is how my frantic travels through Asia got started.

The first grand tour brought me — and my alter ego Suzy Size — to Malaysia, Singapore, Indonesia, Cambodia and Vietnam. I wrote a daily blog about that wonderful trip then. In retrospect, those blog entries were first drafts for the stories that made it into this book.

At a later stage, I wrote only weekly blogs that were more polished than the daily notes, but all text still had to be painstakingly edited for this publication which contains the best stories of Suzy Size in Asia.

To travel with such an eccentric, noisy and shrill heroine is not always easy for me. Remember, I have to carry all those heavy bags containing countless shoes, dresses and fur coats for the old girl... thank god, all these items are just fictional.

But the rest is not fiction. All the stories and encounters happened the way they are described. I hope the readers have as much fun reading them as I had on my trips.

Hans Fritschi

P.S. Since sex-greedy Suzy has seen most of Asia and so many good-looking Asian males, she has extended her trips and is now on a never-ending Gay World Friendship Tour. I, as her loyal servant, have no choice but to follow the good girl all over the world, which can be tiring at times!

CALL BOY
Thailand

01

CALL BOY
A sin-sin situation in Jomtien beach

Suzy Size had been away for a while. But your heroine made a glorious return to good old Pattaya on Friday.

Saturday is beach day. Karl, a retired German, is on his usual lookout in Jomtien beach and takes a closer look. Napoleon, a retired Canadian, complains about his ill health.

Your heroine always rents a chair from the same beach chair provider. Sin, one of the usual 'short timers', is nowhere in sight.

Too bad. Suzy and Sin have a great relationship and an even greater understanding. They never quarrel, because they do not talk to each other more than the absolute essentials: "I am coming sooooon!"

He is from Buriram and has a juicy ass. Most men from Buriram have. The men from Buriram have naturally the best chances to win the annually-held 'Rear of the Year' contest at Copa, one of the many gay bars in Pattaya.

Normally, when Sin is not in Buriram, Switzerland or France — where he has some steady admirers, who all send him money each month — Suzy or Sin just blink at each other in Jomtien beach.

Suzy will get dressed without haste. She packs her towel and the *Economist*. She pays the 40 Baht for her chair and the soda. Other customers pay 50 Baht, but your steady heroine has been coming here for the past 15 years.

And she will walk quietly towards the police box at the entry to gay Pattaya beach. They never walk together. Sin could lose face, being seen together with old Suzy. Everybody, though, knows about this ongoing affair. It has been going on forever. But you do not talk about such private things in Thailand. You just do them.

Only sometimes, when one of his benevolent offshore boyfriends arrives, Sin is not available. Suzy has the highest respect for this arrangement. It is good for all parties involved, a win-win situation.

Either one of the two will arrive first in front of D. D. Inn, a convenient 'short time' hotel. Then they walk in quickly together. They are so discreet here. The concierge hands over the key without any questions asked. The short time fee is 300 Baht, paid instantly. They rush upstairs. A hasty shower and then they jump on each other. Short time takes short time, indeed.

But the problem is, Sin is nowhere on Jomtien beach today. How rude!

Suzy reads her dear *Economist*, freshly bought at Bookazine. Suddenly, she sees an ass that could well be from Buriram. The owner is Khun Soon. He was absent for years, somewhere in Europe. But his cruel former boyfriend has a new boyfriend now.

Before, he was never interested in your heroine. Now he is. Probably needs money. They proceed to the famous D. D. Inn to go to paradise.

Two weeks later Suzy gets a call from Khun Soon at around 10am. "Please, come to my place, I am so horny!"

Of course, Suzy comes.

Since then, Khun Soon calls at least once a week, because he is "very, very horny". A nice way of saying 'I need money'. But his claim must partly be true: when Suzy Size knocks at the door, Khun Soon will be laying naked on the bed with a hard-on. Can anyone fake that?

That is how your heroine finally became a Pattaya call boy. Khun Soon calls at least once a week. And there is ample parking in front of his house. It is so convenient.

Khun Soon has long since become the *Mia Noi* of your Suzy — the 'little wife'. He expects and gets presents, mostly perfumes, when Suzy returns from one of her trips. Like Khun Amorn, Suzy's lazy boyfriend of so many years. But Khun Amorn gets the bigger presents, being *Mia Luang* — the 'major wife'.

Your heroine likes to go on trips. But Suzy Size always returns. She returns to Castelgandolfo, her somewhat pretentious residence outside Pattaya. And to slightly sleazy Jomtien beach.

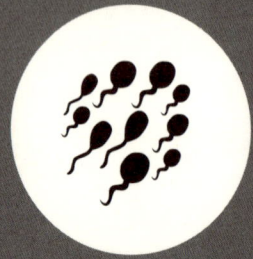

WANDERLUST
Malaysia, Singapore, Indonesia, Cambodia, Vietnam

SUZY SIZE IS IN HEAT

You, gay tourists to Asia, who normally live in the fog or the cold, might not be able to understand why Suzy Size gets bored so quickly these days.

Sitting on Jomtien beach everyday must seem like a dream come true for many of you over there. But your heroine is not happy with this eternal view of hunky volleyball players, talented money boys and all the slightly sleazy gay bars of Pattaya day after day. It is like eating caviar all the time; suddenly you cannot stand it any longer.

Suzy has not been to Singapore, Jakarta or Saigon for years. Wanderlust for Gay Asia has taken Suzy in a tight grip; she is in heat. She has worked out a fine plan to travel with minimal expenses and maximum fun.

First, Suzy checked for some inexpensive flights on Air Asia and found an incredibly cheap promotion from Kuala Lumpur to Yogyakarta for a total of 1,000 Baht (US$32). The important thing with these super cheap promotions is to lock them in immediately as the price might double or triple next day.

Suzy has never been to Yogyakarta and is now looking forward to seeing the world famous Borobodur, the largest ancient Buddhist temple complex in South East Asia. From there she plans to take a train or a bus to Jakarta.

How is gay Jakarta? The last time Suzy was there, she was with her boyfriend (freshly in love) and had no chances or desire for true exploration on the side.

Again on the internet she booked a convenient flight back from Jakarta to Kuala Lumpur for 1,500 Baht (about US$48). And the next day she will fly to Phnom Penh for a ridiculous 2,000 Baht (about US$64).

It will be a Wednesday, so she will have enough time to get a visa for Vietnam before the weekend and take a bus to Saigon (Ho Chi Minh City). The last time she was in Saigon, she was robbed by a Vietnamese hustler. Silly Suzy, be careful!

And from Saigon? No idea yet. Suzy is a big girl, she will probably not get lost.

After securing the major flights, she went to the sleepy train station of Pattaya. Here she bought a train ticket (sleeper) from Bangkok to Georgetown (Penang) in Malaysia for 1,120 Baht (US$36). She has taken this train before, and found it decent and fun.

One night in ugly Penang will be enough. For the day after Penang, Suzy booked a convenient flight to Johor Bahru for 1,000 Baht (US$32). This is the Malaysian town that borders Singapore.

Suzy has never been in Johor Bahru, she hardly even knew that the place existed. But through her internet Gay Guide *www.stickyrice.ws*, she found the website of Artemis massage in Johor Bahru.

And boy oh boy, do they have massage boys! Suzy Size's favourite is definitely hunky Troy, who is "well versed in all massages". Troy, *mon amour*, your Suzy is coming.

Johor Bahru means 'New Jewel'. As soon as your travelling heroine has enough of Johor Bahru, she will hop over to Singapore.

Singapore used to be very boring when it came to gay life, but the city state has relaxed the rules in recent years and Suzy is looking forward to that place as well.

Your heroine will then depart from Singapore in due time to spend a few days in Kuala Lumpur.

She was last there about 18 months ago and was (surprisingly) chased by good-looking young men. Chased for sex, that is, not for money or motherly advice.

If you, gay tourist to Asia, are still a bit confused about the route, the geography or the exact schedule, you must not worry.

You will get it eventually, when you follow this sheer incredible travel tale — good old Suzy takes you by the hand.

A GOOD MAN FROM CHIANG MAI
The surprising encounter in Hua Lampong

Khun Amorn, the boyfriend of so many years, dutifully drives Suzy Size from Pattaya to Bangkok. He has a terrible cold and the doctor has forbidden him to have any alcoholic drinks. That does not make sense to Suzy, but Khun Amorn believes in this treatment. Fine, he drinks too much anyhow.

The train is supposed to leave at 2.45pm from Hua Lampong, the main train station of Bangkok.

Suzy is never late; she is Swiss, where the cuckoo clock could have been invented. (But the honour actually goes to the Black Forest in Germany.)

Suzy is never late, since she always leaves early. The departure time from Castelgandolfo (her somewhat pompous residence slightly outside Pattaya) is set for 11am sharp.

If you have not driven from Pattaya to Bangkok in a while, you will be amazed. The new highway is completely finished. Believe it or not, in less than two hours Suzy arrives in Hua Lampong, which is sadly not such good a place in which to kill time. If only Aqua Pan, the famous gay massage parlour, was open at this hour!

Suzy first checks which platform the train is to depart from. A very friendly official explains in polished English: "Platform 5." The Tourism Authority obviously hires such guys to fool first time visitors about the general foreign language skills of our dear Thai friends.

The train is already here, but your heroine will have to travel on it for another 22 hours, so boarding it now makes no sense.

Suzy could go to the internet café across the square, but she has been on the internet extensively at home. Is there a café to be found anywhere here? Upstairs. Suzy is looking for a stairway, but cannot find it.

Then your heroine comes across a massage place where they offer foot or Thai massages for 200 Baht an hour. Why not?

Suzy wants to be massaged by a man, of course. He shows her into an area with a mat on the floor, separated from the rest of the shop by only a curtain. The guy gives Suzy some very light pants and something like a kimono. Suzy changes and lays down on her back.

The masseur starts by washing her feet, then massaging them. He is very good at it. The slight background music is relaxing. Bit by bit he works himself up her legs.

This guy is excellent with a magic touch and extremely big hands — and boy, he has especially big fingers. Suzy gets a hard-on. Does he notice? Suzy smiles at him, he smiles back and closes his eyes again. This is a very good-looking lad, one of those hunks Suzy likes so much.

When he kneels besides Suzy — now massaging her right arm — he puts her hand right in front of his cock. If Suzy is to stretch her bent fingers, she could probably reach it. Is he deliberately directing her hand there? He still has his eyes closed.

Suzy stretches her fingers and touches that sizeable piece of art. He has a hard-on and obviously likes what Suzy does. His pants are open in no time and that huge surprise is out in the open.

He comes quickly, but in absolute silence. He signals Suzy to come silently as well, after all they are only a curtain away from other customers — discretion is important in Thailand. Then the massage continues, as if nothing had happened.

Suzy asks for his name, age and where he is from. Sai is from Chiang Mai and is 35 years old, but looks like he is 25.

The tip is generous.

STRANGERS ON A TRAIN
A journey to Penang

More and more people board the train, mostly older Thai women. Trains are not popular with the young crowd in Thailand, they have an image of being old-fashioned. And this is true in a way.

The government has never invested much in new trains, except the sky train, the subway in Bangkok and the brand new train to the airport. People prefer buses in general, but good old Suzy still likes trains.

There were two seats facing each other on both sides of the car that could be transformed into upper and lower berths at night.

And here comes Suzy's neighbour, a younger blond English guy in short pants with tantalising blue eyes. He reminds Suzy quite a bit of Michael York, as the bisexual boyfriend of Liza Minelli in *Cabaret*. OK, not really that good-looking (70% of Michael York), but Suzy likes his full sensual lips. They make conversation and Suzy tries to find out if he is her kind.

It just is not clear. He is pleasant and intelligent, but you never know with the English men. They are somewhat undecided, unclear — even the straight ones have that gay touch or that typical English sexual ambiguity.

Looking out of the window, reading the *Economist* and talking to Michael York, time eventually flies.

The conductor not only punches her ticket, he also hands Suzy a list. She has to sign her name beside Car 3, Seat 20, Lower berth — yes, this is indeed where she is sitting.

Then the conductor hands her two 20 Baht notes. Michael York only gets one 20 Baht note. Suzy asks for the reason of this unexpected windfall of US$1.25.

They normally run a train with somewhat wider berths on this route. Since the passengers have paid for that, but Thai Railways is not delivering, they refund part of the price. Less money for the cheaper upper berths, more for the passengers with the more expensive lower berths. It makes some sense, although Suzy would never have known the difference.

When Michael York suddenly mentions his girlfriend, Suzy instantly loses all interest in him.

After dinner, some beers and more of the *Economist*, your heroine retires to her lower berth with a sleeping pill and, *diau gone* (in a little while), sleeps like an angel.

AFTER JOHOR BAHRU, YOU WILL LOVE THE ARCHITECTURE OF PATTAYA
A depressing Jalan Permas suburb full of ravens

Look, you might think this is so easy for Suzy Size. Travelling, having great food or fun with the boys, meeting interesting people all the time and doing a little daily writing about it.

It is easy for you at home; you just open this book, read the newest adventures of your heroine and travel without having to move, without paying any real money, without the least effort.

You do not have to think of how to squeeze your computer plug into a Malaysian socket, which is quite different. Or how to cope when your keyboard at the internet café suddenly writes in Chinese.

Suzy was sitting at Penang airport well on time, having a latté. She was reading a sign — 'Flame Grilled Peri-Peri Chicken' — outside one of the restaurants. What the hell might that be? *Perempuan* was so easy to understand (women) and also *Lelaki* (gents).

These are the boring moments when travelling. You are well on time at an airport and waiting, killing time. Penang had been terrible. Suzy had made no catches, slept badly and felt miserable. Just get out of bloody Penang now.

Suzy moves on to the gate, where she meets flamboyant Penang. All the male ground and flying staff of Air Asia seem to be gay, but Suzy has never seen such a stereotypical tart. This really ugly fat Sikh walks like a caricature of a caricature when he boards the passengers.

This is her last and final impression of Penang.

Suzy is waiting for the bus from Johor Bahru airport to downtown.

The bus ride costs 8 Ringgit (US$2.40) instead of 80 Ringgit (US$24) for a taxi. Stingy Suzy naturally opted for the bus and that is why she has to wait for half an hour. Plenty of time to learn another Malay word: *Ketibaan* (arrivals). Departures are too far away, Suzy cannot read that sign.

Then the bus arrives and takes Suzy to the bus terminal, which is not located downtown. Suzy is glad she has made a hotel reservation on the internet in Penang, otherwise she would be lost now. She boards a taxi and gives the man the address of this convenient downtown hotel. He drives close to what seems to be downtown and then out again. He drives and drives. The outskirts of Johor Bahru seem endless.

Suzy finally arrives at the hotel. It is in a shop house complex in the middle of nowhere, not downtown. This shop house complex is at least 20 times bigger than Paradise Complex, the home of gay Phuket, and at least 20 times shabbier than Paradise Complex.

At least 60% of the units are empty and decaying, while others house cheap restaurants, sleazy night clubs with horrible (female) hookers from all possible Asian countries. No trace of gay Johor Bahru out here in the wilderness, in this depressing Jalan Permas suburb full of ravens. Fucking Johor Bahru!

Is your heroine completely out of her mind? Simply lured here by Troy, a sexy massage boy she saw on the internet? Sweet Pattaya, I love thee so, *lak mak mak*, love much much.

Those who survive Johor Bahru will have great appreciation for the glorious architecture of Pattaya. The hotel itself is not bad; they have wifi, the staff is friendly and the rooms are quiet with all amenities you might want. But the location and the neighbourhood are absolutely horrible.

It takes Suzy half an hour to reach downtown Johor Bahru in a taxi. The Sultan Ibrahim Building is well worth a visit, maybe the Zoo as well. But Suzy is for now more interested in cruising, she has had enough of architecture today. Her gay senses instinctively direct her to Johor Bahru City Square.

Suzy follows a younger Malaysian guy for a while, but he is not interested. Suzy is followed by an older Chinese guy for a while, but she is not interested.

A shrill Tamil *gothoi* (lady boy) "helloooes" at your heroine. Are we back on Pattaya beach road? *Chivit antalay*; life is dangerous, not only in Pattaya, but here too.

IN PRAISE OF GAY JOHOR BAHRU
Paradise finally found

As you know, Suzy Size is never late. And once again she arrives early at the famous Artemis massage in Johor Bahru.

Here in Malaysia taxi drivers can find an address easily, unlike in Thailand with all that confusing 69/69 Moo 69 stuff that is geographically meaningless.

Your delighted heroine saw her wonderful Troy right away. He was having a late lunch at the noodle shop on the ground floor right beside the Artemis building at around 5pm.

Should she sit with him and molest him right away while he was having noodles? Right here and out in the open? Suzy, behave! After all this is a Muslim country where those silly laws introduced by the British are still nominally in force.

Your heroine bounded up the stairs with great expectations. The first impression was most favourable. It is a stylish place and very clean indeed. And lots of good-looking men are employed here.

Chris the owner was not here yet; Artemis stays open till very late and Chris needs some beauty sleep. But Kelvin was already here, he had come over from Singapore where he lives. Suzy had made her appointment via email.

And Suzy Size, despite having only just arrived at Artemis, knew instantly in this magical moment that Kelvin would become a close friend, certainly in this life and probably in the next as well.

Suzy Size was fascinated with Kelvin, but not in the sense that you dirty minded people out there might think. He is admittedly chubby and Suzy Size — chubby herself when a child about half a century ago — just likes sporty hunks like Troy for those kinds of encounters.

But there was no time for hanky panky. Suzy wanted to chat with funny and clever Kelvin, a gay Singaporean who had lived abroad for many years, but was now back in Singapore. Kelvin had set up the excellent website for his friend Chris, the owner of Artemis.

If you, gay tourist to Malaysia, want to go to a place like Artemis, you first and foremost want to know if there is anybody you fancy. And if that somebody can fulfil at least part of your secret desires.

For Suzy Size it had to be her one and almost only Troy, the horniest Johorian ever born. And according to the Artemis website, Troy is "well versed in all massages".

That is exactly what Kelvin provides on that simple but efficient website. Kelvin deliberately chose decent pictures that you may even browse in your straight office environment. Without a knowing eye, one would not think of something indecent, simply that they were sportsmen or just good-looking male models.

The more Suzy talked to Kelvin, the more similarities emerged. They chatted for quite a while. Suddenly, Kelvin asked, "You are not Suzy Size, are you?"

To understand this seemingly silly question, you must know that Suzy Size always travels under the alias of manly Fritzy Frizz. Suzy Size confirmed her real identity to Kelvin, but only to him.

Chris still had not arrived, but called and offered Suzy a free massage while she was waiting. (That is one of the nice perks of this restless reporting from Gay Asia; once in a while you get a freebie.) Under those favourable circumstances, Suzy had to leave Kelvin alone — at least for a short time.

Suzy Size almost fainted when the masseur chosen by (still absent) Chris was not Troy, but a guy named Dayson.

But since beggars cannot be choosers — after all this was a free massage by a professionally-chosen professional — Suzy Size swallowed a tear or two and followed the cute Chinese-looking guy upstairs, where heaven must surely be.

The name of the 22-year-old was easy to remember, even for slightly senile Suzy Size, since it was most conveniently tattooed just above his pretty ass. Only someone with very bad eyesight would have to think of a different trick to remember that name.

Dayson was not so well equipped (as Suzy hoped Troy might be), but he made great use of everything he had.

First he showered with Suzy Size and took the best care of her. She emerged as rosy as a freshly born baby and incredibly clean (the dirty mind unaffected). A body-to-body massage followed, reminding Suzy of the good old times at the bygone Adam and Eve in Pattaya.

You must understand, friends back in Pattaya, Suzy has to write a bit cryptically about this event in Johor Bahru — Malaysia is a Muslim country with ancient laws. Just think of Anwar Ibrahim.

Dayson is a native of Kuala Lumpur and has moved to Johor Bahru for financial reasons; here he can simply earn more money. Singapore is nearby and Artemis boys can hop across the border easily and provide their many services in the privacy of homes or hotel rooms. During the weekends Dayson likes to party in Singapore; gay life seems to be more interesting over there.

It is incredible how much you learn about a person during such a massage. Time just flies, flies, flies.

Chris had arrived in the meantime and for quite a while Suzy stayed and chatted with the owner of the unique Artemis massage parlour and his good friend Kelvin.

And then Suzy left that friendly place and returned to her hotel in that horrible suburb of Johor Bahru — full of uncountable ravens — dreaming all night of horny Johorians such as Troy.

"PLEASE MIND THE PLATFORM GAP."
Suzy arrives at the famous Fragrance Hotel in Singapore

Kelvin, Suzy Size's new friend, had sent a detailed email on how to find her way to Singapore over the Causeway bridge and then by MRT to a station near her hotel. This was very helpful information and without it your heroine would surely have been lost and this glamorous gay trip might have ended abruptly and certainly somewhat prematurely. A bit like premature ejaculation.

For all the copycats, who will in the next 100 years or so follow the steps of Suzy Size and travel on this unique route set out by her, she will tell you how to cross the bridge from Johor Bahru to Singapore.

First you proceed to the Causeway, the crossing point between Malaysia and Singapore. You go through Malaysian immigration. Then you board one of the buses there to Kranji MRT (Mass Rapid Transit) station and buy a ticket for the MRT train.

On the Causeway bridge you will see all these gigantic water pipes. Singapore gets most its water from Malaysia and the contracts are good for another 50 years or so.

Suzy stood in line at Singaporean immigration and was sent back, having not filled in an arrival card. Since they could not find anything negative about Fritzy Frizz, the strict Singaporeans let Suzy Size right in.

At Kranji MRT station a new problem emerged — there was no money changer anywhere in sight. Suzy had only Malaysian Ringgit, US Dollars, Thai Baht, Swiss Francs and Euros, but zero Singapore dollars with which to buy a MRT ticket. She remembered that some of the Singaporean taxi drivers on earlier visits had taken credit card payment, but there was no taxi in sight at fucking Kranji MRT station.

Suzy tried one of her cards at the ATM machine she spotted not too far away. But it was one from Switzerland and to remember the right code was not as easy as to remember Dayson's name. Suzy just tried the code she usually uses for all her cards (if she does not forget to change the given code when a new card is issued).

Out of the machine came 500 Singapore dollars. Miss Size was no longer poor! She was actually too rich now; the ticket machine would not accept any of those high denominations. Suzy bought a bottle of water and could finally purchase one of those valuable MRT tickets.

They have a strange MRT ticket system in Singapore: you have to pay a S$1 deposit for each ticket you purchase, which is refunded if you return it to the machine after arriving at your destination. Aside from this, you will find the system quite easy to understand. Even Suzy Size, who is admittedly a complete technological idiot, managed to find her way.

Just somewhat strange are the constant announcements over the loud speaker. At each and every MRT station, they ask you both in Chinese and English to "Please mind the platform gap".

While staying in Singapore and travelling frquently on the MRT, Suzy Size heard about a million times: "Please mind the platform gap."

In no time, Suzy arrived at Aljunied MRT station. As Kelvin had predicted, from here the taxi cost under S$5 to reach Fragrance Hotel Crystal in 18 Geylang.

THE RED LIGHT DISTRICT OF SINGAPORE
Two handsome apprentice pimps

When Suzy Size arrived at the Fragrance Hotel Crystal in 18 Geylang, they could not find the internet reservation of a guest who had arrived just before your heroine and the man left grumbling. They did, however, find Fritzy Frizz's reservation in no time.

The lobby of Fragrance Hotel Crystal was a bit spartan. They had a safe in the lobby and Suzy had all her diamonds, pearl necklaces and the 12 baht gold chain stored there. Singapore is, after all, a port city and there might be some sexy sailors found — sexy, but AYOR (at your own risk).

Suzy went up to the room which was OK, but certainly not worth

US$74. In Thailand, the hotels are far better value for money than in expensive Singapore.

There was not even a fridge in the room, but a very strange price list at the door. If you want to purchase an ashtray at Fragrance Hotel Crystal, they will charge you S$40. It is a completely ordinary ashtray worth a maximum of half a Singapore dollar.

If you opt for the telephone, it is S$150. The priciest item is the curtain at S$300. No, those things contain no gold and are not designer items from Italy, they are all old and ugly.

It is probably one of those silly warning signs that you find all over Singapore, Suzy thought, and returned to the lobby for a walk around the neighbourhood.

The fact that Suzy had arrived in the red light district of Singapore became definitely clear when she saw an old Chinese man in the lobby, with pitch-black dyed hair and a youngish but ugly whore beside him. He had just booked a room for two hours.

Girls waved constantly at your walking heroine, thinking they were waving at manly Fritzy Frizz. Or their friendly pimps invited Suzy in.

They even have silly sex shops here nowadays, where they sell vibrators and dildos. This very Chinese neighbourhood with small Chinese shop houses, vivid street lights, some tall hotels by the hour, duck restaurants and street whores from Vietnam, China, Thailand and Myanmar — this was not at all like the Singapore Suzy had seen on earlier visits.

This was not the sterile city Suzy knew from Orchard Road. In fact Suzy liked it quite well, it reminded her of home in slightly sleazy Pattaya.

She had a delicious meal of duck and a Tiger beer. She then moved to another one of those simple restaurants, where she chatted with her table neighbours — two elder Chinese gentlemen — and had some affordable beers.

The older one, a 75-year-old, left shortly before midnight with one of the girls; the other shortly after midnight, alone.

On the way back to the hotel, Suzy saw a 24-hour internet café and wondered why would anyone need 24-hour internet access in the Singapore red light district. She entered and went online.

There were bundles of bank notes on the counter. Suzy realised this internet cafe was probably a front for something else. But for what?

They had two young and handsome apprentice pimps here with brute faces and wild tattoos.

Suzy watched them, fascinated, from the corners of her eyes, but did not dare to approach them in any other way.

SEX AND THE (GAY) CITY OF SINGAPORE
Raw revelations at a mall

Your heroine walked through the civilised, but boring, streets of Singapore and found a huge advertisement board for sex.

Suzy was shocked. You could not hang such a sign in Pattaya's Boyztown without causing a commotion or scandal, and the culprit would probably be deported and banned from Thailand for life.

That seems to be the fundamental difference between Thailand and Singapore. In Thailand you do not talk about sex, you just do it. But here in Singapore they hang up advertisement boards that simply read: SEX.

But somebody explained that this was only an abbreviation for an original company name which might really be something like 'Suzy Eve and Xanadu Company Limited', that clearly reads S.E.X.

If you think about it, you have to agree that they are not promoting sex in a senseless or irresponsible way; they only advertise their company — which happens to be a sex shop.

Suzy wanted to go on a hunting spree now. Given the time of the day (late afternoon), Suzy went cruising at Raffles City where people like us not only go for shopping, but friendship — or sex — if you will.

For years, gay Singapore cruisers have used Raffles City. They are so discreet. But Suzy had no problem spotting the gay crowd. Look on the upper floors and wear your biggest smile.

But hunting for gay sex in a Singapore mall can be a tiring pastime, especially if you no longer pass for a spring chicken. And those Singapore malls are awfully well lit and just too bright for your greying Suzy and her many wrinkles.

She gave up and moved to greener pastures, which might be found in the dark rooms of a sauna named Raw Resort. What a name for a gay Singaporean sauna!

SEX AND THE (GAY) CITY OF SINGAPORE II
Raw revelations at a resort

Suzy Size had known about Raw Resort through their website. The two guys pictured on the entrance page really make you want to come, in every respect.

Raw Resort (they have some rooms or barracks as well) is located on a little hill just around Chinatown, where most gay Singaporean hangouts are located. One of the gay Singaporean websites (called Monday or Tuesday or something like that) rates Raw very badly as being filthy.

Suzy Size did not get that impression. Raw is not untidy. Your heroine checked it all and even looked in the dark corners with a flashlight. Look, this is serious reporting, not a joke of some kind! Suzy climbed up and down all the different floors and there was quite a crowd, so Raw must be doing something right for its many returning patrons.

It was just that Suzy did not spot the two good-looking guys from the website. Nor did your restless heroine see anybody nearly as good-looking. This was obviously a bit different from Artemis' website. The gay icon of Johor Bahru shows their boys, who can be met personally on their premises.

Suzy, for example, could have interviewed her beloved Troy for hours and hours and she could even call him over to Singapore now. And the longer she stayed at Raw, the greater the temptation to make that call became.

The gay males of Raw Resort Singapore might all have been brilliant in their own field (like quantum mechanics), but they just were not Suzy Size's cup of coffee. The Chinese were all too mature — Suzy Size has never subscribed to Daddy Magazine, not even the Chinese version. Other patrons looked more like hamsters to Suzy; cute maybe, but she could never have sex with those.

Of course your heroine did not show her negative impressions, she did not want to hurt anyone's feelings. The lovers (and maybe mothers) of those ugly nerds would not be able to understand her anyway. Beauty is in the eyes of the beholder.

SEX AND THE (GAY) CITY OF SINGAPORE III
The gay icon of Singapore

Suzy Size had heard a lot about a gay sauna in Singapore called Club One Seven. Another reliable Singapore taxi had dropped her in front of it. Your heroine entered without further delay and joined the club immediately. Yes, you have to be a member here if you want to use the premises — or rather, the other patrons.

There are no money boys; it is a give-and-take affair between consenting adults, remember that, gay tourist to Asia.

What happens here may theoretically be illegal, but the nowadays more liberal Singaporean government just looks very strongly in the other direction, although they have not yet had the guts to change the silly sodomy laws inherited from the Brits. Even conservative India got rid of them recently.

The premises of Club One Seven are very nice, if you are interested in workouts you will find everything you need.

Suzy, ripe for a beer before any action, could not get one — they do not serve alcohol. Maybe because it is supposed to be a health club? But it is a sex club.

In Babylon Bangkok or in Sansuk Pattaya sauna you get as much booze as you like. Call it a friendship club if you like that better, but it is still a sex club. It is for Singaporean gay sex that Suzy is here. Suzy loves cute Chinese men (amongst others); she is a bit of a 'rice queen'.

It was underwear night. Upstairs, everybody had to wear underwear — at least in the public area. There were some studs and the atmosphere was friendly.

After a short time, Suzy and a tall big Chinese guy were kissing in that French way as if they had known each other for at least a week. Nice big tits that guy had. And a nice big ass. And boy, he really liked grey Suzy. This is always a surprise to Miss Size.

In no time they went to one of the cabins where Suzy enjoyed what he did very much. And your heroine returned the pleasure in a way that is still unspeakable in Singapore.

After Club One Seven, Suzy Size headed to the bars. The gay night life of Singapore all happens in a relatively small neighbourhood (Chinatown); most major places are located within walking distance of each other. That is very convenient for the philandering gay sex tourist.

Yes, Suzy is — in a way — a gay sex tourist; meaning, always open for sex if it happens. Naturally, Suzy prefers to travel to places where there is the chance of sex, the chance of a choice. In America they might call that 'pro choice'.

In Gay Asia, the chances are much better for mature men than in the US or Europe. There is less of the youth craze in Asia. Old age is revered. That is good news for old tarts like your heroine.

After an approximately 20-minute walk, Suzy arrived at 78 Neil Road. But Tantric Bar was a bit too hip for your fast-ageing heroine. It is a place for a younger and cheery crowd that likes to turn night into day, especially during the weekends. But they were very friendly here and told Suzy how to get to Backstage, which is their sister bar.

In her haste (or greed?) to reach Backstage Bar on Temple Street, Suzy forgot to take a close look at Taboo Bar just opposite Tantric, which is often compared to DJ Station (still the most famous gay disco of Bangkok even after all these years). But since Suzy is not really a dancer, she probably missed little.

They let the rainbow flag fly high at Backstage Bar and a friendly young man waved Suzy in from the balcony. It is a friendly meeting place and reminded Suzy a bit of Telephone years ago, when it still was the gay bar to go to in Bangkok. She enjoyed the good atmosphere at Backstage, had a couple of ice cold draft beers for S$10 each (about US$6) and talked to some of the younger friendly Chinese guys there.

The next time, Suzy thought, she would stay at a hotel right in Chinatown. Next time? Yes, Singapore has definitely arrived on the gay world stage and is well worth a visit.

KETIBAAN ANTARABANGSA
International Arrivals

Suzy waved down a taxi in Singapore and told the driver "Changi", adding "Budget Airport" in order not to be driven to the namesake Changi prison.

After all, your heroine could have committed a crime against the ancient laws of Singapore which still ban sodomy. But she was never going to acknowledge such an act, or be caught doing it. (Just a hint for the gay masses that want to copy this trip: do not go to the budget terminal, Air Asia is actually located in Terminal 1.)

Upon arriving at Kuala Lumpur budget airport, Suzy Size further enhanced her Malay language skills by adding *Ketibaan Antarabangsa* (International Arrivals) to her vocabulary.

She was sitting in that freezing cold red airport bus at the *KL Perhentian Bas* (Bus Stand) that should bring her to the *Stesen Sentral* (Main Train Station), which was quite centrally downtown.

But this ungrateful bus just would not leave till it was full. It took ages. Suzy could even add the beautiful words *Ketibaan Dalam Negeri* (Domestic Arrivals) to her growing vocabulary.

In Penang, she had already learned the important word *Lelaki* (Men) from a toilet door. The less important word *Perempuan* (Women) came from the same important source, but next door, of course.

Since this rotten red bus (which was really freezing cold) would not make any move at all, Suzy also learnt *Perlepasan Antarabangsa* (International Departures).

Did life not consist of perpetual *Ketibaan Antarabangsa*? Followed by a series of almost eternal *Perlepasan Antarabangsa*?

Still there was no movement. Suzy read the whole *Simpanan Penumpang* (Customers Copy) of her ticket provided by the Sky Bus Company. Unfortunately it was all in Malay and since they did not offer one of their useful translations, Suzy did not get it this time.

Suzy — this was now very clear — should have taken the yellow bus, which had already left this ugly airport for Stesen Sentral. The yellow bus cost 8 Ringgit, one Ringgit cheaper than the red bus and was probably not as freezing cold. But Suzy was still in this fucking *Perhentian Bas*! This was just not fair. Was Suzy being punished for any wrongdoings, recent or past?

In all innocence, your heroine could not think of any. In the airplane she had fully complied with *Sila Matikan Telefon Bimbit Anda* (Please switch off your handphone). And she had strictly followed *Pasangkan Tali Keledar Keselamatan Semsa Duduk* (Fasten seat belt while seated). She even had refrained from stealing the life vest, not because it was a serious offence, but she just had no use for that ugly yellow thing. Suzy took only calculated risks when travelling. She was *Awas* (Careful) within the airport building where the floor was wet, the sign had warned.

A beautiful blond man sat beside Suzy Size and the bus finally left the *Perhentian Bas* because it was now filled to the last seat.

Looking at this handsome young god, Suzy's heart warmed in this still freezing cold bus to downtown Kuala Lumpur. He was a Swede, headed — like your heroine — for famous Bukit Bintang, the 'Golden Triangle' which also happens to be the most important gay area of Kuala Lumpur.

NO WAR FOR TROY
A passionate poem instead for the dearest of all men

Some of you, gay travellers to Asia, might suspect that Suzy had forgotten all about her beloved Troy by now, whom she almost met at Artemis.

In that taxi, from Stesen Sentral in Kuala Lumpur to Bukit Bintang, Suzy thought about him and their somewhat strange, but also ideal relationship. There had never been a bad word exchanged, nor had any nasty misunderstanding led to a war of words.

As a matter of fact, they had never spoken, which helps in avoiding conflicts. Troy was not going to be a name for another guilt, in order to paraphrase a silly sentence of Max Frisch, an overrated Swiss writer (no, he is not even related to Fritzy Frizz).

As the older amongst us might be aware, in the past there was a prolonged war about Troy, a war about beauty (or a war about sex), and Suzy was very aware of the imminent danger of historical repetition. Such things can happen quickly and when they do, they happen over and over again. Look at Bosnia and all those other shit holes on the Balkan or in the Middle East. Iraq. Afghanistan. Pakistan. How useless are all those wars!

Maybe Chris or even Kelvin were themselves in love with Troy? Was that talented masseur Dayson just a bait, introduced to detract the deep longing, nay, love of Suzy Size for her one and only Troy? It is certainly possible, one cannot rule out anything at this unique Artemis Massage parlour in Johor Bahru.

In this (at least thinkable) gay conspiracy, Suzy could not even rule out that the Swedish guy on the bus was sent deliberately by super dark forces to divert her attention as well. So she did not invite him to share a taxi with her (probably her paying the full bill as usual) when they arrived at Stesen Sentral, and were both in principle going in the same direction.

It was still not too late, Suzy was still in Malaysia and could call

Artemis in Johor Bahru to have them send call boy Troy over to Kuala Lumpur.

It was only twilight. The point of no return would probably be reached when Suzy set foot on Indonesian soil. She was planning to go to Yogyakarta after KL. That was the final point of no return, the real and indefinite goodbye, when it came to matters regarding Troy.

On that very taxi ride from Stesen Sentral to Bukit Bintang, your heroine — in an almost superhuman effort — outlined the one and only poem she ever wrote (and ever intends to write).

She polished it later at the proper premises of McDonald's Bukit Bintang — nowhere else can you get so much inspiration in KL or worldwide, forget the Viennese coffee houses.

Since Suzy Size dislikes poetry in principle, she can promise that this one will remain her only trial on that very wide field upon which many have lost track over the years. Think of German poet Georg Trakl, who became a drug addict. Or perhaps only a drug addict could write such poems? (Just for the record: with this unique poem, Suzy also invented Neo Dadaism.)

Lelak Lelak Troy

Lelak Troy, lelak lelak
Lelak lelak, lelak Troy
Suzy ketibaan antarabangsa Johor Bahru
Lelak Troy ketibaan dalam negeri Johor Bahru
Suzy lak lelak Troy mak mak
Suzy Artemis Johor Bahru

Lelak Troy Artemis Johor Bahru

Awas Chris? Awas Kelvin?

Quidquid id est

Timeo Danaos

Et dona ferentes

Dayson lelak lelak

Troy lelak lelak lelak

Suzy perlepasan antarabangsa Singapora

Troy dalam negeri Johor Bahru

Awas, awas!

Chivit antalay

Awas, awas!

Sila matikan telefon bimbit anda

Awas, awas!

Pasangkan tali keledar keselamatan semsa duduk

Awas, awas!

Suzy perlepasan antarabangsa Kuala Lumpur

Perempuan Suzy lak lelak Troy Johor Bahru

Lelak Troy lak perempuan Suzy Kuala Lumpur

Suzy Kuala Lumpur Bukit Bintang

Lelak Troy, lelak leluk

Awas, awas!

Suzy, diau gone, perlepasan antarabangsa Yogyakarta

Lelak Troy, lelak lelak Johor Bahru

Lelak lelak, lelak Troy

RETURN TO BUKIT BINTANG
The gay hotspot of Malaysia

Look, Suzy knows this well — literature and poems are not for everybody, sex is definitely more interesting for you all. For many, the pair (literature and poems) can be a poisonous mix, acting as an extremely strong sleeping pill — like the infamous knock-out pills used by prostitutes in Pattaya sometimes, when they rob their customers.

But let Suzy Size, in a few words, explain some important aspects of Neo Dadaism. As you all know, Dadaism was developed in Zurich, mainly by German artist refugees, after the devastation of World War I.

Now there is one link: Suzy Size is from Zurich, but is not quite as old as Dadaism itself. And the world — at least in the travelling perspective of Suzy Size — is in much better shape nowadays.

Dadaism is negative in a negative historical environment. Dadaism denies that there is any sense at all. Whereas Neo Dadaism is positive, in a positive historical environment and full of love.

Never was it so simple for the gay tourist to travel on a worldwide scale. And never was it so cheap. This is all due to the internet. To quote Barack Obama: "Yes we can." Or, how Air Asia puts it, "Now, everybody can fly."

Neo Dadaism is therefore full of praise and love for our great gay times and its achievements, and full of love for the universal money boy, who gives all (and more) every day. Troy is therefore the most forceful symbol of hope for the gay masses and not just the little pet boy of Suzy Size.

When Suzy arrived at the booked guesthouse in Bukit Bintang, she was very surprised. The Swede, whom she had met on that freezing cold and endlessly delayed airport bus, was already there. Was this a good or a bad omen?

Suzy had booked that guesthouse in KL from Penang, through the very same website that gave her the accommodation in that fucking dreadful suburb of Johor Bahru full of ravens.

Now this guesthouse in Kuala Lumpur was in a really good location, right in the heart of Bukit Bintang, where the major gay places of that Malaysian capital are located.

Suzy watched the Swede check in. To cut a long story short, it took them 40 minutes to check that young good-looking Swede into a dormitory bed at the guesthouse. Endless were the forms, invoices and explanations that helpless the desk girl gave out or had to fill in.

At first, Suzy took the over-lengthy procedure with humour. She was not in any hurry, even though the boys of Bukit Bintang were waiting. But when it was finally her turn, and it became clear that her room was still not ready at 4pm — and the bitch that still and unrightfully occupied it was nowhere in sight and nobody knew when she would be back, Suzy left the premises of that unwelcoming guesthouse and tried to find more suitable accommodation in the neighbourhood.

Of course, she went to Number Eight Boutique Guest House almost right next door.

THE BOYS OF BUKIT BINTANG
The gay hotspot of Malaysia

What a difference at Number Eight Boutique Guest House! This was a professional check-in, a professional welcome. They only could accommodate Suzy Size for two nights, but at least she had a roof over her precious head and was not forced — like Joseph and pregnant Mary — to look for shelter in a barn.

In no time they had keyed her credit card into the system and deducted the rate for the first night: 155 Ringgit (about US$45). They charge 20 Ringgit more during the weekends and this was undoubtedly a weekend. It is quite customary in Bukit Bintang to charge a surplus during weekends. Well, the demand for rooms is just much higher then, when everybody wants to get laid. It is sort of a vice tax, similar to VAT.

The staff is most friendly at Eight, but one complaint must be made. The TV in the room is not connected to any cable and therefore any channels. It is only connected to a DVD. But both — DVD and TV — could not be connected to electricity. Your heroine complained about this three times and was always assured that something would happen, but nothing ever did.

Right after check in Suzy Size went on a hunting spree to Sungei Wang Plaza, an extremely cruisy Shopping Mall just five minutes from the Eight Hotel.

Suzy passed an interesting square with all those Chinese restaurants. She stopped at a 24-hour convenience store to buy a coke. When she entered, she saw a black guy with a great torso and a big ass.

Naturally, our heroine smiled at that beautiful son of Africa when entering that store. He smiled back and greeted Suzy, although he may have thought he was greeting Fritzy Frizz.

When Suzy came out of said shop, that juicy black stud followed her. He soon caught up and gave her his telephone number. His name was Emanuel and he was from Cameroon.

But then he got an urgent phone call and had to leave immediately. Suzy promised to call him in an hour. But she was a bit wary. The people of Cameroon are very hostile towards any gay stuff.

Well, one should not hold that against poor Emanuel, who probably was a gay refugee and himself a victim of that hostile behavior in Cameroon.

But Suzy remembered her experience in Amsterdam last year, when a friendly black guy that smiled at her so winningly turned out to be a dangerous drug dealer — not a friendly male prostitute.

Suzy continued on her way to Sungei Wang Plaza, where she also saw that Swede cruise, but soon followed a good-looking Malay guy.

His name was Brian, he was working at a hotel. The two entered an elevator. When the other passengers went off, the two stayed on. When the other passengers had left, and your two protagonists were finally alone, Brian got right to the point and asked Suzy Size: "What are you?"

When she did not quite get it, he said: "Top or bottom?"

When Suzy answered "Top", Brian left without a further word and Suzy was instantly very lonesome. But only for a moment. After all, she had so many options in Bukit Bintang.

She had already fetched the number of Emanuel, that horny black guy from Cameroon. She would first go back to Eight Hotel for a rest. From there she could call Emanuel and make a date with him. But that could wait until the next day as well.

She would probably arrange to meet him at Day Thermos, the gay sauna right here in the heart of Bukit Bintang. If this obvious money boy was playing tricks, he would have a hard time robbing Suzy within the premises of Thermos, where they had secure lockers. And there were other possibilities.

She still had the number of Robert, a young horny Chinese guy she had met last year in Sungei Wang. He not only had his nipple, but also his cock pierced, wanted to get fucked, was not after money and spoke English extremely well. A very pleasant short time memory of gay Kuala Lumpur.

But Suzy eventually did neither, at least for the moment. She opted for Blue Boy instead and made the mistake of going there too early.

When Suzy arrived at Blue Boy around 10.30pm, there was hardly anybody there. But that was slowly going to change.

By midnight, Blue Boy had become a great meeting place. Suzy, slightly tipsy from all that rather expensive beer, chatted with Toni, a Chinese guy from Penang who lives in London but had returned to his homeland (not to boring Penang of course) for the holidays.

Then there was Raj, an Indian guy with a huge torso, juicy tits and a big ass. Suzy — who has so far never had sex with an Indian — was very much fascinated by this guy that obviously liked her so much. She had to buy him some beers and did that with great pleasure.

The only irritation was, he was always talking to his brother on the phone, who did not know that he was one of us. But he wanted to touch Suzy and therefore got her to move to the darker parts of Blue Boy.

But there not much was happening. He did not want to kiss or his cock taken out of his pants.

Well, these Indians are mighty conservative, Suzy thought.

He finally let the cat out of the bag and said that he wanted 150 Ringgit for a massage. Suzy would have paid that money without hesitation, but he was pushy and wanted to leave immediately for Suzy's hotel. Suzy was not being pushed, she got his number and told him she would call him next day. She moved to a place near the entrance.

Toni invited Suzy back to his place. But she was not interested in Toni. Shan, a tiny Chinese guy, bought Suzy a beer. They started to kiss deeply in a corner at Blue Boy; it was a nice pastime.

He warned her of Raj, the supposedly Indian guy who really was from Bangladesh and usually robbed his clients, sometimes drugging them first. Not a big surprise for your lucky heroine. Shan asked Suzy to join him at his apartment. Suzy felt too drunk and was not really sexually interested in Shan. She got his number and promised to call him the next day.

Suzy left Blue Boy around 3am and never called Shan.

THE BOYS OF BUKIT BINTANG II
Is there any sexual correctness left?

Suzy loves to walk in cities, even though Asian cities are definitely less made for walking than their European counterparts. But gay Kuala

Lumpur (the Bukit Bintang area) is good for walking. From her hotel, I Yang massage in 201-B Jalan Imbi was within walking distance. According to their website, they had "more than 30 masseurs at your choices".

Your heroine walked around Bukit Bintang and some guy sitting on a bench blinked at her. Suzy looked back and he could not stop blinking.

A tic, the poor guy has a tic, Suzy thought.

But then he followed your heroine, who was well on the way to Jalan Imbi. But she had read the map completely wrong and had to ask for directions.

The blinking guy was now an acquaintance and assistant, and helped Suzy in her search for Jalan Imbi. He was actually a friendly gay guy from Burma. He loved Suzy Size enormously. He wanted to suck the cock of Suzy Size for one hour, he said. He was 35 years old and not after money. But he was a bit smelly and had dandruff. Well, he could shower at the hotel. He begged Suzy to take him to her room.

He said, "We do not often get white wine here." He repeated that remarkable sentence several times. But Suzy was not so convinced. She was mentally and physically well on her way to I Yang, having finally found Jalan Imbi.

Now, standing in front of 201-B Jalan Imbi, there were tough choices to be made. It was about 2pm and the Burmese had to start work at 5pm. The window of opportunity was rapidly closing.

On the one hand, there was this generally nice guy from a country horribly oppressed by ruthless generals. And he loved Suzy so much, he said it over and over again. And they did not get white wine often over here, remember? Was there not a moral obligation for Suzy Size to bang with that oppressed individual?

Is there any sexual correctness left?

Suzy faced a dilemma. If she had a heart of gold, she would take this Burmese gay guy to her hotel and let him have that white wine they do not often get over here. But she was driven by sexual greed. And duty.

Yes, duty. Duty towards the readership of this fine publication. She had to report truthfully and at length about gay Kuala Lumpur, this was her '*raison d'etre*' here.

She explained to the Burmese, she had to go upstairs to I Yang and conduct intensive research. If she was back in five minutes, the wine tasting could take place. If she was not back in five minutes, she was a bit sorry, but very busy.

And up the stairs of 201-B Jalan Imbi she went; one of those typical, ugly shop houses of Kuala Lumpur.

They have one of those interesting photo albums in I Yang. A 25-year-old Chinese guy that reminded your heroine a bit of Goofy (but a sexy Goofy) showed Suzy the working material, the men in the album.

Suzy asked all kinds of silly questions about them, but none of them were actually in at the time. Goofy was the only option, the others would arrive much later or could be arranged via telephone. But right now, it was either Goofy or that Burmese threat downstairs.

The price of a one-hour massage was 70 Ringgit, including masturbation (Goofy volunteered that precious piece of information). If there were 'special services' rendered, the additional price was up to the customer and the masseur.

Suzy was curious and went for it, leaving Burma indefinitely to his sad and isolated fate.

I Yang is a bit run-down — to put it mildly — when it comes to sanitary installations, but Suzy saw no rats and they do have one functional shower. And the massage could start immediately after.

Goofy had the most sensitive fingers you can imagine. But then the door bell rang at I Yang. Goofy had to stop short and open it, since there was no one else there yet.

It was Burma calling. Suzy did not want to see Burma. Burma left. But unruly Burma came back again after a few minutes, interrupting Goofy yet again while he was performing his magic touch. Burma was reprimanded and sent away. The massage could continue in earnest.

Goofy would not kiss, since that was an integral part of 'special services'. Suzy eagerly enquired about 'special services', she was here on a mission to find it all out, remember gay tourist?

Sucking was 100 Ringgit. Fucking 200 Ringgit. Stingy Suzy went for the inclusive hand job.

Goofy became very big himself. He was such a handy man at work. First class technique. Magic, magic Goofy.

Suzy was almost tempted to write another poem, this time for great Goofy. But a promise is a promise and enough is enough.

(Said Rabin and was shot.)

THE BOYS OF BUKIT BINTANG III
It is a crowded planet

The great time in Kuala Lumpur was coming to an end. The next day Suzy Size would have to leave this hospitable place for Yogyakarta. But this morning she first had to change hotels. Eight hotel could only have Suzy for two nights, she had to look for a replacement in the neighbourhood of bullish Bukit Bintang.

Suzy went back to the Replica Inn where she had stayed at before. At 105 Ringgit Suzy got a very good rate, this is a brand new building after all, and the rooms come with a fridge, air conditioning and TV with many channels to choose from.

But are they gay-friendly? In other words, do they allow strangers to come to your room? After all, the programme was 'Banging in Bukit Bintang'.

It is a clear yes. They just have no clue what you might do in your room. They consider your Malaysian companion to be a (harmless) 'friend' and not a sex partner and thus encourage friendship between an older Farang and a younger local. Look at it this way: the older Farang might be able to teach the younger man many, many things. Think of the old Greeks.

Suzy remembered that horny black guy from Cameroon and gave Mr. Emanuel a ring. He remembered Suzy Size instantly.

Suzy asked, what could he do for her? He said, he did not quite know. Suzy asked him if he could give a massage. But he said, he did not know.

Suzy asked more directly, if she could bang with him in her Bukit

Bintang hotel? But the poor lad was shocked. Never ever had anybody spoken to him that way... Suzy therefore concluded that he was a drug dealer after all! She hung up the phone.

It now was time to head over to fantastic Sao Nam Restaurant. Suzy had discovered that delicious Vietnamese restaurant the year before and had dined there several times. They are relatively expensive, but good.

On the way over to the restaurant Suzy passed by the 'Crowded Planet Restaurant', which had indeed been very crowded the day before. It was now completely deserted, because the roof had just collapsed.

Suzy took it as a *memento mori* and moved on for culinary delights — the second best thing (after sex) you can have after such a near death situation.

The food at Sao Nam was excellent. The Vietnamese chef — quite a bitch — was pestering her staff as usual. Suzy found the waiter super cute. What an incredible ass!

His name was Tony and he was from Indonesia. His boyfriend was American. Tony, who had to work late, gave Suzy his phone number and email address.

On her way back from Indonesia, your heroine would stay (a short time with a tight schedule) in Kuala Lumpur again. She then would most certainly bang with Tony and get a piece of that extraordinary ass.

Tony, *mon amour*, you are so lovely!

No more poems, though.

PERLEPASAN ANTABARANGSA
Arrival at Yogyakarta airport

The journey to the LCCT-KLIA and the waiting time till her *Perlepasan Antabarangsa* to Yogyakarta gave Suzy Size yet another opportunity to further enhance her Malay language skills.

Awas, awas! This is written everywhere and rightly so. Remember, gay tourist, this is a crowded planet where roofs can fall instantly and planes can fall too.

Suzy repeated her favourite word as well: *Lelaki*. Lovely *Lelaki*! Was there ever a more beautiful word created in the whole universe?

It was a two-hour and fifty-minute flight from Kuala Lumpur to Yogyakarta, the longest flight on this memorable trip, and at the same time at 1,000 Baht (US$32), the cheapest.

At Adusijiptan Airport (what a pretty name), Suzy emerged from the plane early and proceeded right to the Immigration counter where they issued visas on arrival. The taxi to the hotel was US$6 and Suzy had lost an hour since Yogyakarta is in a different time zone.

Suzy did not come to Yogyakarta for gay encounters or blunt sex, but mainly for the world famous Borobodur, an ancient World Heritage Site. There is no structured gay scene in Yogyakarta, unlike in Kuala Lumpur, Bangkok or Singapore, and Suzy had the lowest expectations regarding the gay life.

A friend had recommended 'Ministry of Coffee' in Jalan Prawirotaman, a friendly coffee house which has several good rooms as well. Suzy had made a reservation and they had confirmed her stay (for Fritzy Frizz).

Jalan Prawirotaman is the backpacker street of Yogyakarta, and thus the recommended area to stay in. Suzy, rejuvenated by a successful trip so far, looked forward to staying in an area where young men from all over the world gather.

When Suzy Size arrived at that very friendly Ministry of Coffee, she was expected and very welcome. The room was good value for money, had a safe for all your heroine's crown jewels, air conditioning, and TV with all the international channels. But there was one disturbing sign just near the reception. It excluded non-guests from entering the rooms of guests.

What if Suzy should unexpectedly find a gay friend in Yogyakarta? Would they go to some forest? Or a public toilet? Or some run-down short time hotel with cockroaches?

SIGNS OF HOPE
Cruising in gay Yogyakarta

Suzy went for one of those wonderful Bintang beers in a place called Via Via in Jalan Prawirotaman. Via Via is a café and a travel agency. They are incredibly friendly and helpful and inexpensive too. Here she bought an air ticket on Air Batavia to Jakarta and a private tour (it is a crowded planet) to the Borobodur next day.

Over a coffee, Suzy sneaked through a publication called *Jogja Ad* and found under 'Service Jogja' the following two interesting ads:

> *"Massage for male travellers, 40 years old and up.
> Call Henry 081..."*

And:

> *"Male therapist for men, and able to guide you during your vacation. Make your tour & holiday fresher & relax. Call Bimo 081..."*

Mr. Henry and Mr. Bimo were clear signs of hope that there was a gay Yogyakarta after all. The people of Yogyakarta cannot be the poorest in the whole of Indonesia since there is some tourism here and some money must trickle down, but they are certainly poor. There were all those old tricycle drivers in Jalan Prawirotaman competing to service Suzy Size and take her on a city tour, your heroine finally gave in and in the end doubled the ridiculously low price that that poor driver had asked for.

Yogyakarta is acclaimed as one of the more beautiful cities in Indonesia, but Suzy Size was little impressed. She saw a completely naked, mentally disturbed, filthy woman somewhere in the centre of town and nobody gave a shit about her. Your heroine discovered little beauty in Yogyakarta. It was not as bad as in that horrible suburb of Johor Bahru, but Pattaya is certainly much more tidy in comparison.

And if you look for decent food in Yogyakarta, you have to search for a long time; the recommended gourmet restaurant in this city is definitely McDonald's in the Matahari Shopping Mall. That says it all.

The Matahari Shopping Mall is interesting for cruising, especially in the evenings and on the weekends. But for once, old Suzy Size had not come to Yogyakarta for the gay night life, and had (for once) no sexual expectations.

Your heroine headed back to Jalan Prawirotaman and arrived at the Ministry of Coffee just in time before a heavy downpour. There were about six young backpackers at the Ministry of Coffee, all working on their laptops connected to the internet via wifi. They were sorting out their pictures, making airline reservations or writing down their precious impressions of the day in a diary. They made hotel reservations or skyped somebody. But they never talked to each other. How could one ever travel before the internet?

Suzy surfed a bit on the net like everyone else and went out for dinner. The rain was over and Suzy walked up and down Jalan Prawirotaman several times before she finally entered Gading Resto right next to her hotel.

It was a lucky choice, indeed.

MEETING A SAD SAILOR
Cruising (and landing) in gay Yogyakarta II

When Suzy Size entered Gading Resto, she went there because of the food; your heroine was mighty hungry. She did not have her gaydar on and was not looking for sex, believe it or not.

It is an universally acknowledged fact: go to the Philippines, Malaysia or Indonesia and you will only get horrible local food. Suzy looked through the menu at Gading Resto in Jalan Prawirotaman and thought about what to order. What could they least mess up in the kitchen?

Your heroine had ordered one of those delicious Bintang beers and was drinking it while she made up her mind. *Bami Goreng? Nasi Goreng? Awas, awas!* They had more or less the same ingredients here as in Thailand, but the results were completely different — horrible.

Suzy had chosen Resto Gading for its menu. It looked the least terrible in the entire Jalan Prawirotaman. And there were some other guests, which was a bit reassuring. Why the hell had Suzy left wonderful Pattaya? There was an abundance of fine restaurants to choose from back there. Was your heroine on the verge of becoming homesick?

Suzy was just mighty hungry. She finally ordered fried rice with seafood, not too difficult to prepare. When the food came, Suzy was well onto her second Bintang. The food was edible, but the Bintang certainly helped. But the waiter, Suzy suddenly realised, was very cute. How could such a good-looking man serve such horrible food?

Suzy started a conversation with him — or was it an inquisition? In no time she knew his whole life story.

His name was Rico, he was 28 years old, and he was from a hamlet in Sumatra with two or five million inhabitants, Suzy had never even heard of the name.

He had come to Yogyakarta in order to study the fine trade of sailing at the local academy. He had finished his education, but sadly enough, had never been able to find any employment on a ship. He was a bit like a fish without water, a beached whale, forced to walk on the land as a waiter.

What a sad sailor. But he did have a mighty beautiful smile. He had a 'friend' in Jakarta whom he visited often. What kind of relationship might this be?

And he was going to leave Yogyakarta in two more days in order to work in Brunei. He mentioned that he still needed some money to pay for the passage. Tonight he worked the night shift, but the next day he was on day shift which ended at 6pm.

"And then you go home to your dear wife?" Suzy tested the waters, so to speak, if you are familiar with nautical — not naughty — terms.

"No wife," the sad sailor responded instantly.

Suzy invited him to come to the Ministry of Coffee next day. He was obviously eager to come. The high tip may have helped.

BOROBODUR IS A BIT BORING
Cruising gay Yogyakarta III

Suzy Size sat at the Ministry of Coffee in Yogyakarta having a latté, her morning routine while cruising the internet. But then she googled 'Borobodur' and found the following piece of information:

"The Borobodur Temple complex is one of the greatest monuments in the world. It is of uncertain age, but thought to have been built between the end of the seventh and beginning of the eighth century AD. For about a century and a half it was the spiritual centre of Buddhism in Java, then it was lost until its rediscovery in the eighteenth century.

The structure, composed of 55,000 square metres of lava rock, is erected on a hill in the form of a stepped-pyramid of six rectangular stories, three circular terraces and a central stupa forming the summit. The whole structure is in the form of a lotus, the sacred flower of Buddha."

Off to Borobodur your heroine went. She entered the *Masuk*

(entrance) and climbed up the structure. She thought this to be a pretty place and yes, probably OK, to visit once in a lifetime.

But Angkor Wat was much better. Even Wat Phou in Champasak province (Laos) impressed your heroine much more. Borobodur bored Suzy a bit. She almost wished she was back at sacred Artemis, being entertained by her hero Troy — who else?

She was glad that some male beauties graced the slightly boring Borobodur with their presence. Your heroine did not molest them, even though the thought was tempting. But she stole some pictures of them: what a harmless pastime. And someone — pure madness — stole her picture (naturally in the disguise of manly Fritzy Frizz).

1 hour and 45 minutes was more than enough for Borobodur. Suzy could actually have easily died without ever having seen this World Heritage Site, but such things you always only know after a trip.

The driver was quite surprised to have your heroine return after such a short time, ordinary people seem to stay much longer. But your heroine is not ordinary.

When Rico entered the Ministry of Coffee shortly after 6pm, Suzy was sitting in the café having another latté and surfing the web. He had a seat and they talked about unimportant stuff for a while to keep up the façade of being good old friends.

Suzy was now going to try to take Rico to her room. But there was this disturbing sign just near the reception which explicitly forbid non-guests from entering the rooms. It was a very big sign and most certainly here for good reasons.

But the female receptionist, who wore a head scarf, no veil though, did not issue a *fatwa*, instead giving Suzy Size a big smile of approval when she walked by with Rico.

Bravo, they do obviously discriminate against straight people at the Ministry of Coffee, not allowing horrible female hustlers into the rooms. One must congratulate them on their straight-unfriendly policy! But they surely do promote pure male-male friendship with an unknowing smile.

The rest of the story you can probably imagine yourself. Except the size of Rico. It even surprised your old size-queen!

THOSE WHO TRAVEL DO TAKE RISKS
In search of gay Jakarta

At the Adusijiptan Airport in Yogyakarta they are terribly careless: they still let you bring in your own bottled water! Apparently they have, in their incredible naivety or ignorance, not even heard of the dangers of water.

In other more civilised countries, they will take your dangerous drinking water away from you immediately when you go through the security check, and look at you as if you are a dirty terrorist, because that bloody water can explode. Suzy thinks the hydrogen car is based on that technical principle. But in Yogyakarta, they are not in fear. *Awas, awas.*

You can even bring your suntan lotion onto the plane. Or your tooth paste. Or your aftershave. Or your liquor. They are very backward at Adusijiptan Airport in Yogyakarta.

Suzy feared for her life taking that dirt cheap Batavia flight to Jakarta, but the train would have taken seven hours. The plane looked OK from the outside, but Suzy is no aviation expert.

It even started on time and, to cut a long story short, all the terrible and frightening fears of Suzy Size were in vain. She arrived safely at Jakarta airport. The water bottles did not explode. And in no time her checked-in baggage arrived as well. Your heroine had to show her baggage tag while leaving the restricted area, thus proving she was the rightful owner of her many bags.

Suzy enquired about a taxi to the centre of town. The first answer was 180,000 Rupees (about US$18), but that guy went down to 160,000. The next started at 140,000 Rupees.

When Suzy was outside the restricted part of the terminal building, droves of taxi drivers wanted to drive your heroine. The prices started at 200,000 Rupees this time. One would do it for 120,000 and the stingy part of Suzy opted for him.

The other Malay drivers got mad at the Chinese-looking guy who undercut them. Suzy remembered that amok is a Malay word. (*Wanderlust*, *Schadenfreude* and *Kindergarten* are German words that made it into the vocabulary of any world language.) Would they run amok?

Suzy followed her driver to the car. A brand new Toyota, the seats were still wrapped in plastic to preserve its pristine look. But there was no taxi sign.

Suzy had obviously gone with a freelance taxi driver. How stupid. How careless. He could drive her anywhere. He could drive to some abandoned house, haunted by the ghosts of all the other passengers he had already murdered there. He could drive to a lonely rice field or some weird woods. He might not murder Suzy Size outright, but leave her naked there with nothing left, completely helpless. She had everything with her. The jewels, all the 15 Baht gold chains, cash, passport and several credit cards.

This man could be a mass murderer. Even in comparably civilised Bangkok, a taxi driver had been murdering several of his passengers whom he had picked up from the airport. How much more was this possible in impoverished, unruly Indonesia? But the man did not look like a mass murderer. What do mass murderers look like anyhow?

To appease him, Suzy paid all the highway fees. The driver returned the change immediately each time. That might have been a clever move to disguise his criminal mass murderer nature.

Did Pol Pot look like a mass murderer? Was there not even a slight resemblance between Pol Pot and this Jakartan driver? Suzy worried much, so much. But finally your heroine arrived at her designated hotel.

The driver now suddenly wanted 140,000 Rupees instead of the 120,000 agreed upon. Suzy paid gladly. She was so happy to have survived. Otherwise, she would never have met M. Idris.

AN OASIS OF LOVE AND PEACE IN A HORRIBLE CITY
In search of gay Jakarta II

Suzy Size had made a reservation at Cemara 6 Galeri via email and M. Idris, the manager, had confirmed her room. At 200,000 Rupees (roughly US$20), this was dirt cheap.

The few well-designed rooms of Cemara 6 Galeri are grouped around a little court with a café. To reach the café, you have to pass the namesake high-class gallery. They give you free wifi and throw in breakfast for this bargain price. The place is located in Jalan H. O. S. Cokroaminoto. If you are familiar with Jakarta, there are some embassies nearby, the Goethe Institut and private villas. Within 5 minutes you are in Jalan Jaksa, the backpacker street every taxi driver will be able to find.

Your heroine was received by a wonderful, gorgeous young man and decided that he must be M. Idris, the stunning manager that had confirmed her room. He spoke very little English (most Indonesians speak very little English).

Suzy knew little factual stuff about M. Idris. She was not even sure that this gorgeous guy was indeed M. Idris, the manager. But who cares? M. Idris is between 23 and 25 years of age, probably about 1.70 metres tall. He has the fairest of faces, remarkable eyes and the most sensual lips.

M. Idris, *M. Idris*, *M. Idris*, does not the sound of his name alone evoke something benign? M. Idris always smiled his killer smile, which was not vulgar at all, but pure and innocent. Suzy could not take her eyes from M. Idris.

She had to call him to her room several times, the air conditioning stopped working after half an hour more than once. M. Iris solved the problem each and every time.

But Suzy Size was shy (for once). She did not dare to corrupt this wonderful M. Idris. If he was gay, he certainly had a true and only lover. Suzy did not want to interfere and thus destroy such an ideal relationship, nor did she think she really had a chance to drag pure

M. Idris into her filthy arms. If he was not gay, she did not want to embarrass him or tempt him with a financial offer that he might not be able to resist. M. Idris was clearly out of reach for Suzy Size; her chastity — a really rare event — was instantly restored.

There was a problem with the lock of her room. Who solved the problem? M. Idris!

But when Suzy returned from her first round of discovery that fateful evening, M. Idris was gone. He had three days off and Suzy never saw him again. Your careless heroine has not even taken a picture of M. Idris for her intimate memoirs.

But the picture of M. Idris is deeply locked in the heart of Suzy Size, her heart only. And this finally proves that she has a heart, after all.

JAKARTA, THE HORRIBLE CITY
In search of gay Jakarta III

Suzy Size should have stayed in her room in Jakarta. Maybe she even should have stayed in her bed.

She could have called William over, who is, according to his ad in the *Jakarta Post*, a 'Top model' and available 24 hours. Or Abie, who was, despite the girlish name, a man as well, and available 24 hours. Or Alik. Or Dino. Or Glen. All available 24 hours.

But no, she did not want to lose face in the eyes of benign M. Idris, by inviting a male prostitute over. Your doomed heroine had to go out and walk around in horrible Jakarta. Besides, she was on a mission. Therefore she has to investigate, she may not make up anything.

First your heroine walked through Jalan Jaksa, the backpacker street of Jakarta. It is a dump, but then the whole city is a dump. Jalan Jaksa, in a way, is less of a dump than the rest of Jakarta.

Suzy will have all her Jakarta meals in Jalan Jaksa, in a horrible German restaurant called Yaudah, where they have *Eleanor Rigby* on permanent repeat. The food at Yaudah is OK, they have German sausages and Swiss Rosti. But the atmosphere is lethal.

9M, THE HEAVENLY GAY PLACE IN HELLISH JAKARTA
In search of gay Jakarta IV

In Jakarta, Suzy Size should not have walked anywhere, she should have taken a taxi the first thing in the morning to take her to Jalan Talang Betutu 4. That is where 9M, the gay heaven of Jakarta, is located. Once your heroine had reached that almost sacred address, she was so eager to get inside.

You can always have a first glance at 9M via their website. But be warned: they do not show their crown jewels, their massage boys, on the internet like Artemis does. But you get an impression of the nicely decorated place which is very clean indeed, with nine massage rooms in total — which explains the name 9M.

Suzy Size was received by the good-looking and polished Assistant Manager Angga, who enquired about the needs of your heroine. Was Miss Size also visiting the sauna or only here for a massage?

"Only massage."

One of those photo albums was presented. They really should have their models online, even though none would match Troy or M. Idris naturally, but that is very difficult indeed. Some of the best-looking were working the morning shift. It was now the night shift.

Suzy finally found a protagonist and paid the fee of 225,000 Rupees (about US$22.50). She could have used Visa or Master Card as well, but the tip for the masseur would probably have to be cash (between 200,000 and 300,000 Rupees).

Should Suzy bore you with another one of her dull sex stories? Should she describe in details his ass, cock, nipples and lips? And what he could do? And what he could not do? Are you never getting tired of all that sex stuff?

Suzy is getting tired of being your gay guinea pig. She misses the peace and quiet of her Castelgandolfo residence. She misses dull Jomtien beach. She certainly would appreciate a fine dinner at home. She would like to play with Lilly, the Golden Retriever. Or watch a high-class movie from the Suzy Size Movie Collection. And she would certainly like to know if her plants in the garden are still alive. Do you, boyfriend of so many years, water them well, Khun Amorn?

So, if you have to go to Jakarta, make sure you go to 9M. But think twice before going to horrible Jakarta at all.

When Suzy left hospitable 9M, she asked Angga a few more questions regarding other gay places in Jakarta, especially for directions to 'The New Moonlight'.

But this good-looking and polished young man, Assistant Manager of such a respectable and laudable institution as 9M, a delightful gay brothel, warned Suzy Size not to visit 'The New Moonlight'. As the main reason, he quoted from the leading internet Gay Guide *www.stickyrice.ws*: "Many money boys."

Grateful for this motherly and immensely precious advice, Suzy Size went straight to bed.

GLORIOUS GAY KUALA LUMPUR
No time for sex though this time

Suzy Size had made a mistake. She had booked the cheapest of three Air Asia flights from hellish Jakarta to heavenly Kuala Lumpur and was to arrive there at 11.15pm. But, when the plane arrived on time in Kuala Lumpur, there was a heavy downpour.

Suzy does not understand why, but it took them one and a half hours to bring the luggage to the terminal. Maybe the workers just did not want to get wet? Maybe the rain would ruin their coiffure?

Then there was the tiring bus ride to Stesen Sentral. Followed by a taxi ride to Bukit Bintang — the driver wanted 30 Ringgit; Suzy bargained him down to 20 Ringgit, but the real price would have been 8 Ringgit.

Suzy checked into Replica Inn at 2am. Now it was too late to call Tony, the sexy waiter of Sao Nam Restaurant with that juicy ass. Suzy Size was very hungry and left Replica Inn for urgent food. When she crossed the road to the square with all those Chinese restaurants, she saw a very good-looking guy with a Farang about Suzy's age. They were obviously a gay couple, and they were boarding a taxi.

Suzy smiled at that guy anyhow, pure routine. When she looked back the Farang had left with the taxi and Mr. Sim followed Suzy Size.

Mr. Sim had been out partying with his Farang friend, but the Farang was leaving early next morning. Mr. Sim now had a blank spot on his agenda.

He soon asked Suzy Size, "What are you?" Suzy had learnt what that meant. Brian had asked the same question in the elevator. And even Goofy wanted to know after his handjob, probably just out of curiosity. This seems to be a vital question in Kuala Lumpur.

When Suzy answered "Top", she hit the jackpot, because Sim was a bottom. He wanted to go to Suzy Size's hotel room immediately. But poor Suzy was so hungry and quite tired too.

She invited Sim to join her for some of those tantalising chicken wings over at one of the Chinese restaurants, but he had already eaten, and was only hungry for sex. Suzy proposed that he visit her at her hotel room in the morning. Sim was thinking about that tempting proposal when he left.

But, alas, cruel Mr. Sim! Nobody came the next morning to the lonesome hotel room of Suzy Size. Suzy Size's latest visit to gay Kuala Lumpur thus ended with a mighty sad and sombre notion.

Our distressed heroine left without consolation the next morning for Phnom Penh, to discover gay Cambodia.

THE GAY HEROES OF PHNOM PENH
Staying at Manor House

Another two-hour flight from Kuala Lumpur to Phnom Penh. For the very last time, Suzy could read that glorious word *Lelak* written on a toilet door.

And then, after some prolonged and deep thoughts about Troy, which are omitted here for reasons of obscenity, Suzy Size arrived at the airport of the Cambodian capital, Phnom Penh. The Visa on Arrival is still US$20 and is issued quickly (bring a picture). The taxi to town costs US$9.

The Cambodian driver resembled Stan Laurel from afar. He did not quite know where Manor House was, where Suzy Size had made a reservation for two nights, but consulted a map with utmost diligence.

At every red light he consulted the map again. With his fingers he went over the roads he had to take. Suzy thought Stan Laurel would never find Manor House, but vicious Suzy was proven wrong; he finally stopped right in front of the gate.

Manor House is conveniently located just around the corner from the Independence Monument, has a pool and is like an oasis in the Cambodian capital. There were two other guests from Pattaya, who stayed at Manor House with their Thai boyfriends. The faces seemed to be familiar and after some chatting Suzy found that they used the same beach chair providers in Jomtien beach. It is a small (gay) world.

Suzy headed for the FCCC (Foreign Correspondents Club of

Cambodia). They have a reliable and intelligent travel agent there and Suzy enquired about a visa for Vietnam. The regular visa was US$34; express service was US$40, which meant that Suzy could pick it up in the evening the next day and board the Mekong Express Bus the following morning as planned. She bought the ticket for US$12 right there too and went upstairs for a pizza and a beer overlooking the Tonle Sap river. The FCCC is crowded these days, never before were there so many tourists coming to Cambodia.

But it is not a gay meeting place, be warned gay tourist. You should visit anyhow, it has become a landmark since the 1990s and even hardened homosexuals should not always seek sex.

THE GAY HEROES OF PHNOM PENH II
Blue, Blue Chilli and salty Salt Lounge

There were basically two main gay bars in Phnom Penh: Salt Lounge and Blue Chilli. After dinner at the FCCC, Suzy Size headed right to Salt Lounge which was walking distance away (Blue Chilli is, too).

There are bars with interesting names just beside Salt Lounge, for instance Babylon and 69 Bar, but be warned: they are straight bars where all kind of strange vices are promoted. *Awas, awas*!

Suzy Size saved her soul by entering Salt Lounge in haste. The staff here was friendly and spoke some English as well, the atmosphere was very relaxed. But Suzy Size was suddenly saddened. There was that nice young guy she had met about six months ago and he was extremely friendly with... an old gay Japanese horror tart!

Suzy became extremely jealous at once. Could this brute not have waited a few months in chastity for your divine heroine to come back? Was this seemingly nice and diligent business student (as he had portrayed himself before) really a horny sex monster and notorious Phnom Penh money boy? Was there no real love to be found in gay Phnom Penh any longer?

When that certain young man went to the toilet, your heroine immediately followed him to have a few stern words. But, alas, insult was added to injury during this conversation — he could not even remember flamboyant Miss Size.

Severely saddened Suzy Size naturally left sombre Salt Lounge with a somewhat salty taste on her tongue and went straight over to Blue Chilli. (It should not come as a surprise to you, gay tourist to Cambodia, Salt Lounge has closed down in the meantime and does not exist any longer. There seems to be a sort of poetic justice...)

What a difference! At Blue Chilli, Suzy was seated at a table outside with three good-looking gay Phnom Penh heroes. Two of them she already knew from previous visits. And she had obviously made an impression on them — they both remembered her! Naturally the trio was treated to several beers.

The new acquaintance spoke hardly any language besides Cambodian, whereas the two older friends spoke some English and one spoke Thai quite well. They all offered Suzy a good massage, but flattered Suzy refused. The Mekong Express was to be taken early in the morning and your heroine needed a good night's sleep. One of the boys even drove her to the hotel and was tipped for that simple service rendered.

The Mekong Express had promised to pick up Suzy Size at Manor House in the morning. But they were late. Suzy got nervous. She did not want to miss her dear Mekong Express. She asked the receptionist to call them.

He (no, she) did, but with grumbling. It was, as she said, not her duty to do so, since Suzy had not bought the ticket at the hotel reception.

Honey, you are surely a bitchy sour ass. Suzy told her something about service and explained that she had not even known they were selling tickets for the Mekong Express.

But then the minibus soon arrived and brought your heroine right to the bus terminal. Miss Saigon, Miss Size is coming!

ON THE MIGHTY MEKONG EXPRESS
Miss Saigon, Miss Size is coming

Suzy Size got on the Mekong Express and fell instantly in love with the super-cute bus attendant. With utmost grace he handed out the cold towels. Then every passenger got a bottle of wonderful water from his very well-sized hands. And finally Beauregard handed out a lunch box with a sweet and a meat cake. Lovely meat cake, Beauregard. He certainly was in the same league as Troy and M. Idris.

But the best were his super lovely announcements, first in Khmer, then in English: "Lady and Gentlemen."

Not that the content was interesting, but it was the beautiful way he talked. So polished, so well behaved; a Cambodian Sunday school boy with an apple ass.

Early on in the journey, Beauregard also distributed the paperwork for the border; the Immigration Card for Vietnam, a duty declaration. Later, he would take all the passports and get all his loyal passengers through customs, that motherly Mekong Express saint. But that was much later.

It is a bit of a long ride to take the Mekong Express from Phnom Penh to Saigon. It took seven and a half hours. Beauregard told Suzy and the other passengers how many square kilometres each Cambodian province they passed had, how many villages and hamlets, but Suzy does not remember a thing, listening instead to Beauregard's wonderful voice.

At one stage the Mekong Express boarded a ferry and crossed — who would have thought? — the mighty Mekong.

At one bottleneck (road construction), the hapless Mekong Express was delayed for almost an hour. Suzy killed time watching the landscape fly by (when the bus was not stuck) and she talked to her neighbour while watching the godly apple ass of fair Beauregard, who often walked back and forth in the air-conditioned and comfortable Mekong Express.

Suzy Size's neighbour was an American, about 60 years of age, travelling alone too. Suzy suspected he was gay. She asked all kind of questions in order to find out.

He was not married. He used to work as a flight attendant, now retired. He was living in Fort Lauderdale. All indicators said yes.

But your heroine just watched his eyes when Beauregard walked by. And, bingo! If this guy was not gay, Suzy was straight too.

MR. NO-BULLSHIT
A gay son of Saigon

Heartbroken Suzy Size had to say goodbye to beautiful Beauregard when the Mekong Express reached its bus terminal in the well-known Pham Ngu Lao street of Saigon, or Ho Chi Minh City. This is a very central location, more or less opposite the New World Hotel and within walking distance to the Opera and the other major points of interest.

Suzy Size took her small backpack and the laptop (she had left the heavy stuff in Phnom Penh) and crossed the street. She entered Freedom Hotel and let them show her the rooms. They had two room categories, one for US$17, the other for US$22.

Can you imagine? Stingy Suzy took the more expensive one that was more spacious. And Freedom Hotel turned out to be gay-friendly, there was not the least problem taking male visitors to the room. They probably just had no clue what was happening, just like at the Ministry of Coffee in Yogyakarta.

Suzy went for a walk in search of gay Saigon. Parallel to Pham Ngu Lao street she found Bui Vien, which is the backpacker street of Saigon. Suzy had a wonderful Saigon beer in Quan Huong Vy restaurant on Pham Ngu Lao street. The waiter there was quite good-looking and the local beer (the food too) costs nearly nothing. This is generally true in Saigon.

The place proved to be perfect to watch the Saigon world pass by. Suzy decided this would become her headquarters. But not now; as long as there was any light left to philander, later.

The cute waiter said, when Suzy got up to leave, "You will be back at 8pm." Suzy found that remark, this prophecy, a bit odd.

Saigon, contrary to Jakarta, is made for walking, even though it is quite difficult to cross the roads at times with all those motorcycles, cars and bicycles. Suzy had a look at Ben Thanh Market, walked by the Opera, the Continental hotel and lit a candle in the Cathedral for good luck.

Saigon is a nice place, reminiscent of Paris in an exotic way. But if Suzy Size had to choose between Saigon and Hanoi, where she had recently been, she would prefer Hanoi which is less nervous than Saigon, less phony, cooler, and more reserved. Saigon is more of a whore than Hanoi.

Suzy walked by a small and inexpensive restaurant near the Opera and studied the menu. The waiters opened the door and tried to lure your heroine inside. Suzy had a look.

Even though it was only 6.30pm, there were some Vietnamese guests sitting at the table behind the window, studying the menu. This was a good sign, Suzy thought. She entered the place and ordered spring rolls and glass noodles with shrimps.

As soon as she had placed the order, she realised the couple in the window was phony. The restaurant had seated two employees there as extras, so the restaurant would not look so empty.

How clever, Suzy thought. The employees were highly professional in luring tourists into the place. Now Suzy, sitting there, had become part of the setting. If there were Vietnamese and Farang customers, the place looked good in the eyes of tourists walking by. And with Suzy abused as bait, the place was full within an hour. Then the Vietnamese extras could give up their position at the window and go do some serious work.

The food, by the way, was quite good and Suzy was amused by the little ploy. Suzy had all the time in the world. Slowly, taking many detours after dinner, she went back for a Saigon beer in Quan Huong Vy restaurant on Pham Ngu Lao.

It was now about 10pm. The sexy waiter who had predicted Suzy would be back was gone, but now Mr. No-Bullshit was here. He was quite obviously gay and after a very short time invited Suzy to join him at his table.

Suzy Size joined Canh at his table in Quan Huong Vy restaurant. He was a talkative guy, obviously gay with a blond streak in his hair and the sun tattooed on his left upper arm. He was 38 and a bit fat, not really Suzy Size's type, but he was funny at first and Suzy Size wanted to exploit his (hopefully) deep knowledge about gay Saigon.

Canh loved Suzy instantly, which was definitely a one-sided thing. He kissed your heroine right there in public, and Suzy was suddenly a bit shy. He wanted to come to your heroine's room right away, but Suzy was reluctant and actually much more interested in some cool Saigon beers. His favourite words were "no bullshit" and he worked in the nail business. In that nail business, no hammers are required, the human nails were Canh's business, who said it was easy to beautify them.

Wanting to know which hotel Suzy stayed at, he gave her a ride back on his motorcycle and promised to meet her at noon the next day for a Saigon City tour.

Suzy was sitting at the internet at the lobby of the Freedom hotel when Canh entered at 10am. He was really eager to take Suzy Size around and had not waited until noon.

But Suzy, burnt once in Saigon, was careful. She had been robbed during her last visit about ten years ago by a hustler, who actually looked a bit like Canh. She had gone with him to a short time hotel. Suzy had no clue where in Saigon she was, since he had driven your naïve heroine there on his motorcycle.

Oddly enough, the door of the room had no lock. When the hustler and Suzy took a shower, your heroine became suspicious. She looked back into the room and saw somebody taking off with her wallet. Suzy screamed and made a big fuss. Long negotiations followed. She finally got her wallet back, but US$150 was missing.

Canh first took Suzy to a shopping centre, where she bought him an expensive hairspray when he looked so sadly at it. Then he wanted to take her to a public swimming pool, they are notoriously cruisy in Vietnam. But Suzy had left her swimming things in the suitcase in Phnom Penh.

Canh said he knew of a 'beautiful place', but since he was running low on fuel, Suzy bought him a full tank. He drove for almost an hour through the ugly suburbs of Saigon, until he reached a silly Vietnamese amusement park.

Suzy was little amused, but had a look at the nonsense anyhow. Canh finally let the cat out of the bag. His nail business brought him 400,000 Dong a month, but now he had to pay his rent, which was 500,000 Dong.

He said he had had a severe fight with his landlord that morning and could be evicted any moment. When he threatened to commit suicide for the second time in that amusement park, Suzy encouraged him to enter the adjacent crocodile farm immediately and end his earthly misery at once. After all, his life was hardly sustainable at the given income and expenditure gap. And, if he really felt so miserable, why not end it all, once and forever?

But Canh just would not join the crocodiles. He begged Suzy for a soft loan. Suzy promised him 300,000 Dong (US$25) for his services as a tour guide and Canh graciously accepted, but promised to pay Suzy back, if she ever returned to Saigon. "No bullshit," Canh said once more.

Now Suzy wanted to see something interesting. She asked Canh to drive her to Cholon, the Chinatown of Saigon. He did not understand; where did Suzy Size want to go? Suzy pronounced Cholon like Cologne, the German city. But Canh had no clue.

When Suzy wrote Cholon on a piece of paper, he finally got it, but pronounced it completely differently. If you pronounce Cholon in the most vulgar way you can think of, you may be close to the proper pronunciation — which is even more vulgar.

But taking obvious Canh to conservative Cholon was perhaps not the brightest of ideas. All those backward Chinese merchants looked at Canh with unhidden disgust, bewilderedment and open mouths.

Walking through Cholon with Canh was a bit like walking through Afghanistan with a pink pet poodle with the Taliban still in power. Shy Suzy pretended not to know him that well.

A GAY SON OF HANOI, LIVING AND WORKING IN SAIGON
Meeting Heintje or Rambo

Suzy Size had dinner in an Indian Restaurant in Bui Vien, the backpacker street right behind her hotel. The food was horrible, but dirt cheap. She had a table overlooking Bui Vien.

There were a lot of young men around with their bicycles, making noises with a little metal instrument and thus advertising their massage services. There were so many, it was almost like Jomtien beach, but in an urban context. They all were eager to make eye contact and — once established — they would come back time and again to sell their massage services.

After dinner Suzy strolled up and down Bui Vien and was approached by several massage boys, all in their twenties. They offered a massage at ridiculously low prices, which could not include a happy ending. Suzy was at first reluctant to take any of them, she did not like hassles about money afterwards, possible threats and troubles in general. One little guy was very insistent.

He chased Suzy Size up and down Bui Vien. From afar he reminded your heroine a bit of Heintje, a Dutch kid, who was a sentimental singing wunderkind, TV and movie star in Germany during the 1970s when Suzy was still young, so young.

Suzy Size spoke to insistent Heintje, who spoke some English, but fortunately would not sing, at least in the streets of Saigon. After all, she had always wanted to go to bed with Heintje during puberty.

She told him she would take him to her room, but wanted no trouble. Heintje agreed on the proposed terms, followed Suzy and parked his bike in the court of the hotel, explained his profession to the reception, deposited his ID and was allowed to enter Suzy's room without delay. They have very orderly procedures here in Saigon, almost like in good old Pattaya.

Heintje, although small, had the body of a miniature Rambo. The two protagonists went to work immediately and Heintje/Rambo obviously knew what he was doing. They both went to paradise in the same few seconds.

After that Heintje/Rambo gave a good health massage and left trouble-free after he was rewarded as promised. He was from Hanoi and had come to work — far away from home — in this service-oriented profession in Saigon. When Suzy asked him if he was gay, he innocently answered, he did not know. The terminology meant nothing to him.

Well, Suzy thinks, she knows. Lovely, lovely Heintje.

👬

Suzy returned to Quan Huong Vy restaurant for some Saigon beers. Canh was there too and asked Suzy if she wanted to go to some discos. Suzy preferred her headquarters at Quan Huong Vy.

Heintje/Rambo drove by several times. Then Heintje/Rambo brought a colleague, who would not move from his observation spot nearby. Obviously he wanted to give Suzy another 'massage'.

Canh noticed the interest Suzy Size had caused and sternly warned your heroine never to go with any of those massage boys. No bullshit, they only caused troubles. They were all from the North and therefore not trustworthy. One of the waiters agreed. Against the will and advice of his dear mother, he had dared to marry a girl from Hanoi. This marriage was a clear failure. Was that not proof enough?

Never trust anybody from the North, you are doomed if you do. They are all crooks and gangsters. And they are greedy, too. Now, so many decades after the fall of Saigon, this seems to still be the common perception. Another interesting note: the massage boys of Pattaya come from the poor Northeast, the Saigon massage boys come from the poor North.

The next day, Suzy Size went back to Quan Huong Vy restaurant, her Saigon headquarters, on that Saturday afternoon to read the *Economist*. She just had found a copy at the kiosk of the New World Hotel. Forced by heavy rain to stay there longer than initially planned, she could not help but have four bottles of delicious and light Saigon beer.

The cute waiter whom she had met on the first day in Saigon was there too. Remember, he had predicted Suzy would be back at 8pm at Quan Huong Vy restaurant that very first day in Saigon? But now she understood why: his daily shift ended at that time.

And when Suzy left, he promised he would visit your heroine after work at her private quarters at the Freedom Hotel. Suzy even skipped the circus, which was in town, to wait for Mr. Chin in her room.

But bad, bad Mr. Chin did not keep his promise. He never showed up and Suzy Size — who had waited for him almost eternally — was severely saddened once again.

Mr. Chin, by the way, is a Saigon native; he clearly is from the South of Vietnam, not from that so terrible North.

AN EPISODE ALMOST FREE OF GAY STUFF
Is Switzerland near Scotland?

You may think Suzy Size makes up all these stories, but they all really happened. Suzy has no fantasy at all and could never invent a thing.

So therefore you must believe your travelling heroine, when she tells you beloved Beauregard was at the bus terminal of the mighty Mekong Express when Suzy got there, early as always.

But alas, he was not wearing the orange silk uniform of the bus attendants, he was only helping the company to board the many passengers. A girl was the bus attendant this time — and she did a great job too, if you allow such a sexist remark for once.

Be warned, gay tourist: this is going to be the least gay episode of this whole trip, so if you do not like such shallow stuff, better skip it and go to the next chapter of the book.

The bus trip back to Phnom Penh was unspectacular. The nice female bus attendant took care of her clients even more efficiently — if this is possible at all — than beloved Beauregard. They had the forms for the Visa on Arrival and the passengers of the Mekong Express could pass the Cambodian border without delay, wait at the nearby restaurant on Cambodian soil until all the paperwork was done and then get the passports back when the bus was rolling towards Phnom Penh.

There was a remarkable five-year-old Asian boy in the seat just in front of Suzy Size. His name was Adam and he spoke English very well and was very talkative. He befriended your heroine instantly, even though she normally pretends to hate children.

But he was so funny, so playful and full of life, the thick anti-children walls around the hardened heart of Suzy Size melted as quickly as the glaciers in her home country. He had a little plastic plane and flew with it around the world on his bus seat. Suzy felt old and definitely inferior.

Unlike Adam, she had to first book all those flights through the internet, then go to all those airports, then board all those planes, then find the way to a hotel, before finding a friend. Adam could do all of that from his bus seat.

You might have guessed, old Suzy was getting tired of all that travelling, she was on the verge of getting homesick. She missed the boyfriend of so many years for nonsensical discussions and the *Mia Noi* for solid and uninhibited sex. And, yes, she severely missed even old Jomtien beach and sleazy Pattaya in general. Even the architecture.

When she reached Phnom Penh, she travelled to Manor House and later had dinner with a straight friend from Pattaya who was here on a sex stop-over. But Suzy did not seek more pleasures of the flesh in Phnom Penh and went to bed early. She had been here just so recently, there was no need to prove anything.

The next morning, your heroine was once again picked up by the Mekong Express and boarded a bus to Siem Reap. The bus attendant was the same efficient girl who had been on the bus from Saigon the day before.

The bus ride to Siem Reap took 6 hours and during the lunch break,

Suzy sat at the table of a friendly Cambodian couple. The man spoke English quite well and Suzy wanted to know all about his life. He had a lot of land in Along Veng, the home place of Pol Pot.

But he was not a mass murderer; he planted trees on his land, which is a bit nicer. At 32 years of age he had just married his 25-year-old wife three months ago and had already managed to get her pregnant!

Those hardened heterosexuals really like to bang like rabbits; it is quite shocking for gallant gays like us indeed. His question to Suzy Size was interesting too: "Is Switzerland near Scotland?"

"In a way," your seasoned traveller answered.

RETURN TO FRIENDLY EI8HT ROOMS
Why does Fritzy Frizz have no girlfriend?

After arriving at the bus terminal in Siem Reap, Suzy Size took a *tuk tuk* and directed it to Ei8ht Rooms Guest House where your heroine had previously stayed.

Ei8ht Rooms is conveniently located just within walking distance from the old centre of town with all the restaurants, pubs and bars. It is definitely gay-friendly, if not gay, and the least expensive of the many such hotels in Siem Reap. They only have eight rooms — you understand the name now, gay tourist — and Suzy Size, who had not bothered to make a reservation, was really lucky to get the eighth or very last one.

Suzy decided it was now time for a refreshing Angkor beer in the late afternoon and headed to Linga Bar. The beer was was served in an ice bucket like champagne. Suzy Size was at ease with herself and the world, sitting at wonderful Linga when a boy about 14 years of age approached her, wanting to sell some post cards.

Suzy did not want to buy any post cards. Then he asked your heroine, or rather, Fritzy Frizz: "Do you have a girlfriend?"

"No", was her honest and natural answer, she was after all sitting in a well-known Siem Reap gay bar.

"You know why you do not have a girl friend?"

"No?"

"Because you do not buy my post cards."

Suddenly, Suzy Size remembered having met the boy before. During her previous visit to Siem Reap, she had had a coffee at another place and was approached by this genius junior salesman then. He had asked the same question. And Suzy told him what he would ask next: "How many inhabitants does Switzerland have?"

The answer would be: 8,856,341 minus 1. Suzy knew she would never get rid of this clever and insistent young man and handed him his US$2 ransom at once. And he kept his part of the deal: he left immediately and did not return.

LINGA, LINGA, LINGA
The gay night life of Siem Reap

Suzy Size had dinner at Le Bistro de Paris in Siem Reap. First of all, their name cards were on display at Ei8ht Rooms (which certainly is suspicious) and secondly, she had eaten there previously. Never change a winning horse.

Suzy suspects the owner of Le Bistro de Paris to be gay as well, since he was briefly visited by a stunning Cambodian guy when Suzy paid her bill. Overwhelmed by sexual greed, she had to follow that sexy guy when he left Le Bistro. What would you have done, gay tourist?

But alas, another big disappointment, he drove away on his motorcycle and was never seen again. When Suzy Size entered Linga again, she was received with a friendly atmosphere. She ordered a cold Angkor, of course.

Your heroine has seen the temples of Angkor about 15 or 20 times, she had no desire to go there again this time. But in the liquid form, Angkor remained very attractive. Suzy Size was soon surrounded by interested young men.

You know what could happen next, fellow gay tourist? Suzy will buy one a drink. Then the two new friends will jump on the motorcycle of that lad. They will drive to nearby Ei8ht Rooms and do their routine. Then Suzy would return to Linga.

At least two other guests of Ei8ht Rooms were now at Linga too. The gay scene of Siem Reap is small but nice. Suzy made conversation with other guests, the manager and a Vietnamese boy, who wanted to be fucked by Suzy Size, but your heroine was far too tired. And she had had almost enough of this restless gay tour through five Asian countries.

Like ET she definitely wanted to go home, sweet home, which happens to be in passionate Pattaya.

ODYSSEUS COMES HOME
Gay Pattaya, my love!

Suzy Size had arranged for a taxi at the reception of Ei8ht Rooms the night before and the driver was there punctually in the morning. The price had not changed since the last visit, it was still US$35 to drive to the Cambodian-Thai border in Poipet or Aranyaprathet respectively.

The road had been completed and the whole drive now took only one and a half hours. The very first time your heroine drove the same route, it took 12 hours in a four-wheel drive.

The casinos are still here and so are the coolies, who drag all the merchandise on their carts across the border. Nobody wants to stay in Poipet any longer. Suzy Size handed her last Cambodian Riel to a beggar and went through Thai Immigration, posing as Fritzy Frizz.

In Thailand, your heroine got a taxi which brought her in three hours and for 3,000 Baht (US$96) to Castelgandolfo, her landmark residence slightly outside of Pattaya.

It was a memorable trip, Suzy concluded, she liked it very much. Sitting on her terrace with a Campari Orange as a sundowner, overlooking the swimming pool and fish pond, your heroine's thoughts wandered back to Hua Lamphong, where her trip had started with an unforgettable massage.

Then she went right back to Artemis, the pearl of gay Johor Bahru (New Jewel). She thought of Chris, Kelvin, Dayson and beloved Troy. But Troy had recently vanished from the Artemis website and saddened Suzy had nervously asked Kelvin — in a hastily written email — for the reason of this sudden and unexpected disappearance.

It came as deep shock when Kelvin wrote: "Troy is gone. He was stirring up some trouble by demanding more than two times the amount in tips from customers and was very destructive."

But Suzy Size had to take another devastating revelation, which broke her heart: "Besides, he's not as blessed down there as we had hoped."

As she sat on her terrace with a Campari Orange, Suzy Size's thoughts flew back to gay Singapore, to Backstage Bar and Club One Seven.

To Kuala Lumpur, the gay hotspot of Asia, where wonderful men in great abundance can be found in blessed Bukit Bintang.

Then to Yogyakarta and somewhat boring Borobodur.

Jakarta, the horrible city, where wonderful M. Idris had to live.

Gay Phom Penh and a terrible insult at Salt Lounge.

Beloved Beauregard on the mighty Mekong Express.

Canh and Heintje and the terrible, long lasting North-South divide in Vietnam.

And finally, gay Siem Reap where many lingams loom.

Tomorrow was Saturday and your heroine would go to good old Jomtien beach. She would park her car in Jomtien Complex, pass the busy construction sites of more and more ugly buildings.

Then Suzy Size would buy the *Economist* at Bookazine. She would talk to Karl on his usual Jomtien watch post and tell him everything about her unforgettable trip. Napoleon would sit near Suzy Size, complain about his ill health and the boring *Pattaya Mail*, each issue hitting another new low.

And maybe one of the steady boys would be in Jomtien beach and your happy heroine might retreat for a short time to D. D. Inn.

Home, sweet home!

Is there a better place on earth than Pattaya?

HUGO
Thailand

03

HUGO IS DEAD AND MADAM MABOLO IS BACK IN JOMTIEN BEACH
Lives — Well spent and wasted ones

Before leaving Pattaya again for another trip, Suzy Size put her house and garden in order. She had hired the younger brother of her boyfriend as a temporary gardener and brought him in from Nong Khai. And — in contrast with Khun Amorn — he really did a good job, was diligent and hardworking, even though his attention was partly diverted for things that are top priorities on Khun Amorn's agenda.

Some fish swam away during the recent heavy rains, when the pond was overflowing. Khun Amorn did something to prevent it and installed a wooden fence where the overflow took place.

Fish breeding is very close to his heart; it is not hard work, it is auspicious and in the end you can even eat those tasty beasts. They are already fat and when Khun Amorn ordered his young brother to catch some with a net, he caught more than wanted and threw some back.

Suzy had to wait several weeks until the second water pump was properly installed, whereas Khun Amorn had his fish lamp up and running in no time: when twilight sets in, the neon light over the water starts to shine automatically, attracting all kinds of insects which eventually fall in the pond and thus serve as involuntary fish food.

Two contrary concepts of life:

Suzy Size sets targets and deadlines and sticks to them, very

Swiss. She plans. If she has achieved something today, she can achieve something else tomorrow.

Khun Amorn's concept of life is totally different. Like most Thais, he does not believe in plans or hard and constant work, but thinks it is most important to choose the right, auspicious moment for anything undertaken. Tomorrow almost always seems to be the better day, if hard work is involved.

Buddhist *Tamboon* (doing good things) is of foremost importance, because it will help the individual in his next life. And one should always try to have *sanook* — fun.

Eating (for instance *Som Tam*, papaya salad) is *sanook*, cooking, partying, talking, sex, all *sanook*. *Sanook* is why Thailand is such a fun place to come to, why the living is so easy for visitors. You just have to get the priorities right in life.

Having sex with an old Western tart is *sanook*, after all. Going on a free drinking spree with him is *sanook*, too. And in the low season there is plenty of quality time to spend with the friends from the same Isarn region by gambling which — without doubt — is *sanook* as well. *Sanook* for Suzy is sitting in Jomtien beach and watching all those guys go by.

There is that Dutch couple over there that lives in Grand Condotel. One of them is a few years older than the other and they look completely alike, clones.

Now they have found a young Thai man that is an Asian version of the two Dutch guys. Suzy Size would love to borrow the young man (who is visibly well-endowed) for a little while, but has no chance at the moment; the two Dutch narcissists watch their catch day and night.

You can almost always find your heroine reading a book on Jomtien beach — looking up once in a while to make her important observations: a juicy ass over there, a pretty face here and a big cock passing by.

A friend brought her a book from Switzerland, the latest and last of Hugo Loetscher, who died just before his 80th birthday. He was a world-famous writer, in Switzerland at least. Suzy has known him for over 30 years.

In the beginning he tried to get your then so young heroine into his bed at the hunting grounds of Odeon Cafe, but with no success. About 16 years ago, he paid her a visit in Bangkok and they went to the infamous Babylon sauna together. Hugo was so fat then; two towels could hardly hide his crown jewels.

The last time she met him was about five years ago, at Grand Café in Zurich where he usually had coffee. Hugo was a great talker; funny, witty and quick. They talked for several hours, Hugo much more than disciple Suzy.

"Mabolo, Mabolo, you want Mabolo?"

Suzy had not heard the old Thai saleswoman trying to sell her smuggled merchandise for at least ten years in Jomtien. Then, when she still smoked, she always bought those cheaper Marlboros from this benevolent, friendly woman

She has aged, of course, who has not? Where might she have been all those years? Probably went home to farm, as if her time in Pattaya never existed. And now, she was back and picking up where she left off, working the trade as she always did, stoically walking the beach every day.

"Mabolo, Mabolo, you want Mabolo?"

Suzy read the last book of Hugo Loetscher quickly on Jomtien beach. It is titled *War meine Zeit meine Zeit* (Was my time my time). Hugo reflects about his life, his upbringing in a working-class family, his personal development, the political and historical environment of his times, his native city, the world and his many travels all over the world. He tries to find the essence of his life.

Hugo Loetscher certainly had a full life; he made the best use of it and his abilities. His last book is quite bad, though. Only little does he talk about his gay life in it. He does not hide the fact, but he is not very talkative about it either.

Suzy is probably not the only one that would have loved to hear more about that.

"Mabolo, Mabolo, you want Mabolo?"

Napoleon, who spent even more years on Jomtien than your heroine and pretends to know just about everything, explains to Suzy why Madam Mabolo seems to have been gone for so long: she had spent ten years in prison. No, silly Suzy, not for selling smuggled cigarettes! According to Napoleon, one night she murdered her husband in Jomtien beach with a knife when she was drunk.

Ah, lives... well spent and wasted ones.

"Mabolo, Mabolo, you want Mabolo?"

OF SUPERMAN AND LESS SUPERB MEN
Macau, Hong Kong, Manila, Taipei

04

GAY MACAU IS A BIT BORING, BUT ALSO A RATHER DANGEROUS PLACE

Once again Suzy Size is full of praise for Air Asia. The two-and-a-half-hour flight from Bangkok to Macau was only 2,700 Baht (about US$86). They were punctual and a cute, obviously-gay flight attendant smiled knowingly and was very friendly towards your heroine, who devoured (and stripped) him with her greedy eyes.

While Suzy was waiting for her luggage, she saw an older Farang with a hunky and gorgeous Filipino and was instantly struck by intensive sexual envy (*Sexualneid*, as Freud probably would have called it).

But, such is life, the unequal couple got their luggage much faster than Suzy, left the baggage claim area of the airport and was never seen again.

Suzy withdrew some cash from the airport ATM and boarded a taxi from Macau International, which is built on reclaimed land just beside Taipa island. She arrived at Best Western Taipa Hotel in no time. She had booked that hotel through some internet site since there are no gay hotels in Macau. And a search on relevant gay websites did not reveal one Macau-based escort, any gay bar or gay sauna, but only a gay (owned) wine shop. Who needs a gay wine shop?

The Best Western turned out to be a good choice as room 1313 was OK (typical dull international charm), but more importantly, the guests there get a magnetic door card and can easily bring friends to the room.

Suzy Size likes walking and for that Taipa (and Macau in general) is ideal; the temperature is moderate, but it is advisable to carry an umbrella.

Taipa village is a well-preserved Portuguese settlement, charming and authentic. You really feel like you're walking in a village in Portugal, but one mainly inhabited by Chinese (that seem to pose as Portuguese).

The food in the restaurants is typical Portuguese cuisine. Suzy had dinner twice in a restaurant at the main square of Taipa village, which could have well been moved here by magic from the Lisbon Barrio Alto.

Your delighted heroine had roast veal (veal is hard to find in good old Pattaya) on her first visit and mussels the next time, and felt as if she were in heaven. Another reason for the newfound happiness of Suzy: wine is relatively cheap in Macau; due to its Portuguese heritage, it is taxed less here as compared to Thailand.

The next day, Suzy Size continued her walks through Taipa Village and then visited the phony Venetian, which is the biggest casino on Taipa, but also one of the biggest in Macau as a whole.

It adopts the Venice theme with campaniles and other architectural highlights of that wonderful Italian city, but sadly enough, no seductively handsome Tadzio can be seen anywhere. It is kitsch as kitsch can be; grossly overbuilt and absolutely tasteless like most casinos in the world.

Macau is much more expensive than Pattaya, but not as expensive as Hong Kong. One good thing those silly casinos provide is free transportation. Most of them have shuttles and by boarding one, Suzy was over at the Macau Ferry in no time. There she boarded another freebie to the Sands, another of Macau's big casinos.

Did you know that Macau has overtaken Las Vegas some years

ago when it comes to casino revenue? Those Chinese all seem to be gambling addicts. There are some hypocritical signs such as 'Do not risk more than you can afford', but these are only for decoration.

Suzy did not even use the free token given to her at the Sands, but left that dangerous place immediately in order to explore the more genuine parts of Macau.

Your heroine has only been here once before and that must have been about 20 years ago. The place has changed dramatically. An unseen gambling boom has ignited a construction boom; casinos are everywhere. The most pretentious one is the Grand Lisboa. This huge golden kitschy building dominates the skyline of Macau.

Climb up the hill to the Portuguese fortress (Monte Fort) like old Suzy Size did and overlook the mess. Grand Lisboa — like a gigantic golden phallus — blocks the view to the harbour; the old canons at Monte Fort are now directed right at it. And then walk through the old part of town where you once again experience that Mediterranean flair.

If you like sweets, there are plenty of bake shops which offer all kinds of specialties, the most famous the Portuguese egg tart. Suzy, who normally has no sweet tooth, liked that tart very much.

You will probably end where you started your walk, at Largo de Senado, which is the main square of the old part of town and really impressive. Especially for gay Macau visitors, since this is the principal cruising area. It is best on Saturdays and Sundays when the many workers from the Philippines meet here, chatting the day away with their compatriots and obviously looking for fun.

Alas, Suzy had come here on a Tuesday! But even on that day

it did not take a lot of staring until your heroine was approached. But, my goodness, that lad was really ugly, almost completely bald. And he was from Iraq, a hairy (body) beast as well.

Suzy showed no interest at all, actually she was rather afraid and instead moved to another watch post on wonderful Largo de Senado. There was a group of three Filipinos nearby and Suzy Size was tempted to make contact with them...

When Suzy Size bolted her hotel door, Ricardo had already helped himself with a beer from the fridge. The sex that followed was extremely dull. Ricardo did nothing but lie down and get a blowjob; dead meat. No kissing allowed, he was a complete macho. His thing, by the way, was not very impressive.

And when Suzy Size handed over the HK$400 (about US$50) agreed upon, he wanted more. Your heroine refused. But then sweet Ricardo took out a knife from his pocket and put it right at Suzy's throat. Before Ricardo left with all the cash, he tied Suzy to the bed with a string conveniently cut from the curtains...

Suzy Size woke up from her nightmare the next morning with a sore throat. She was sweating. She should not have puffed so many cigarettes last night in that nice pub in Taipa Village.

Going over her nightmare again, she was mighty happy she had only been tempted to contact those Filipinos at Largo de Senado, but had not really done so in the end.

When she was on the verge of starting a conversation with those boys, the one that looked like the boss of the gang was approached by the police. He did not have his passport with him, but spoke into his handphone and a few minutes later, an accomplice brought his passport from a side street. He was handed a fine anyhow. That looked all very suspicious. And, at second glance, the other boys there did not look very nice as well.

Suzy boarded a taxi, went right over to Taipa, had some beers at that nice pub and smoked too much. She slept alone. Probably for the best.

GREAT (BUT EXPENSIVE) GAY HONG KONG I
Arrival at a hotel prison cell

Suzy Size boarded a taxi which took her to the Ferry Terminal of Macau. For HK$140 (about US$19) she bought a ticket and arrived in Kowloon an hour later, just opposite Hong Kong island. Your heroine had booked a hotel that was well affordable and looked alright on the internet.

When Suzy reached Nathan Road (which is within walking distance from the China Ferry Terminal at Victoria Harbour) she saw the ugly building in which her hotel was located right away. Just looking at the run-down building explained the unusually low Hong Kong price of roughly US$37 for a single bedroom with its own bathroom, TV and wireless internet connection in USA Hotel.

Suzy queued outside the elevator to Mirador Mansion. There were many backpackers waiting and it took a long time for it to finally arrive.

Suzy was the last passenger to enter that antique elevator, but the first to exit at Floor 13. She was therefore the first at the reception on that barren corridor.

The check-in went fine; they found the reservation for Fritzy Frizz, and they were not really unfriendly, just a bit rough as they have always been in Hong Kong. They asked Fritzy if it was OK that the room had no windows. And Fritzy replied in a manly manner (deepest voice possible), "Yes."

An elder guy took Suzy Size down to the fifth floor where that marvel of a room was. The corridors on Floor 5 were equally filthy as those on Floor 13.

Suzy Size has stayed at many hotels all over the world, but this room was certainly the smallest ever. It was more like a train berth. Or it could be characterised as a toilet with bed.

Any prison cell in a civilised country is bigger. But everything was there, as advertised. A TV hung from the ceiling over the bed, where the feet are. Wireless internet was available 24 hours — when Suzy sat on the bed, she barely managed to open her laptop on her knees. They had squeezed in a small bathroom with a working shower and toilet. And everything was brand new, only the building was old.

After shedding a tear or two, Suzy Size decided to give it a try and it was not that bad in the end.

GREAT (BUT EXPENSIVE) GAY HONG KONG II
All Boys Club, Wally Matt, Central Escalator

When Suzy Size had visited Hong Kong for the first and only time more than 20 years ago, she had hated it. Too many rude Chinese, horrible traffic, constant noise, the lack of gay life — all those factors contributed to her unfavourable view of this hectic city. (And she was still a small town girl then.)

This time around your heroine had a ball and enjoyed every minute of her two stays (two days on the way to Manila and Taipei, two days on the way back).

First of all, it was quite cold in Hong Kong, which is ideal for walking and a welcome change if you live in hot Thailand.

That tiny, tiny hotel room of your heroine was very close to ABC Sauna and New Wally Matt, and on the very first night in Hong Kong, Suzy Size entered the premises of ABC, which stands for All Boys Club. A French guy entered together with your heroine and complained that he had a hard time finding that place. The French always complain.

Suzy soon found a protagonist and started fooling around with that long-haired Chinese boy of maybe 25 years of age somewhere in a dark corner of a corridor. But, alas, that horrible French queen wanted to get part of the meat and interfered with her greedy hands. That gorgeous boy would not have this, of course, and disappeared.

Now the French horror queen concentrated on Suzy Size, who really had not travelled all the way to Hong Kong to have some oily French fries, and she took off as well.

Not long after, she found another performer and did some gymnastics with him in one of the cubicles. After coming, he left as quickly as he had come and sore Suzy Size was alone again, slightly dissatisfied. But then she reconnected with the first one and this time they went into a cubicle immediately.

It was not the greatest sex Suzy had ever had, but a nice way of getting welcomed in Hong Kong. You need not be a renowned psychologist to conclude: if Suzy Size gets laid in any given city, she likes it.

After Suzy Size had mastered her Hong Kong ABC, she moved further to New Wally Matt Lounge, just a few steps away. This was going to be headquarters during her entire stay in Hong Kong.

The Carlsberg is served ice-cold here; the company of nice gentlemen is splendid, too. It is easy to start a conversation at Wally Matt; a funny and cheery crowd comes here and most speak English well. Many Chinese men come here, mainly potato queens.

Suzy got several invitations to spend the night and was even followed by one to the toilet once, to do it right there, but did not particularly feel like it.

She would have gone with beautiful Paul, a Filipino who obviously knew he had the looks, but never was approached by him in that respect and therefore labelled him in her most private thoughts as a conceited cheesy pet poodle.

Your heroine tried three times to lure the Tiger — a call boy — to her hotel room by phone (she likes to ride tigers), but it never worked out, he never made it. Maybe he was afraid, insecure or just shy to meet your flamboyant heroine. Fucking Tiger!

The days in Hong Kong passed quickly by walking up and down the streets, taking the ferry across Victoria Harbour from Kowloon to the Hong Kong side, driving around in those funny double-deck trams, tasting the local food and looking for gay places — which is a convenient way of getting to know a city.

Suzy found the locations of Propaganda, Hunk Sauna and all the other places, but only entered Central Escalator and is now a distinguished member of that very friendly Sauna Club. Your heroine liked it there, because she got laid again — Suzy Size is so predictable!

GAY MANILA DAYS I
This city is still a dangerous dump

The easiest way for Suzy Size to reach Hong Kong airport from her hotel near Nathan Road was to take bus 21 for HK$33 (have your exact fare ready).

The flight on Philippine Airlines to Manila was full of Philippine maids, who are euphemistically called Domestic Helpers (or DH). In the Philippines they use abbreviations for everything, like COMELEC for Commission for Elections, or CB for Call Boy, even if he is just an ordinary street hustler, but CB definitely sounds more elegant.

It took ages to get her luggage at lousy Benigno Aquino International Airport. Suzy Size was sweating a lot and finally packed her leather jacket (badly needed in chilly Hong Kong) into her backpack.

Not only did it take an hour to get her luggage, getting a decent metered taxi took another hour in that Manila heat. After losing his way and thus adding a considerable amount to the fare, the driver stopped right in front of Manila Manor Hotel, which offered a discount of 50% for every second night, if paid in advance and by cash. Suzy opted for the Superior room, which was OK after they repaired the fridge.

They do not trust their guests at that hotel; Suzy Size had to sign a written declaration that there were 2 cushions, 1 fridge, 1 bedcover, 2 glasses, 2 towels, 1 ashtray, 1 telephone, etc. in the room.

When Suzy Size left two days later, they checked the room for all those items, then issued Suzy a receipt at the reception which was to be handed over to the guard at the door 8 metres away: he otherwise would not have let your heroine out.

Manila is under siege, armed guards are everywhere. You cannot enter any shopping mall or elevated train station without a body and bag search. And they are racists. They do not check Farangs nearly as well as their brown brothers and sisters.

The first thing to do in Manila (or Malate where you will naturally stay, since most of the gay places are there) is to take a walk through Rizal Park. It is named after the local national hero, Dr. Jose Rizal, who fought for independence and is revered almost like a god by newspaper columnists, politicians and specialised local historians. I guess after Marcos, Aquino, Estrada and glorious Gloria there are not many politicians left to look up to?

On the way to Rizal Park, Suzy Size took a look at Robinsons Place, a relatively new shopping mall. It is very cruisy on Fridays and Saturdays and Suzy was approached in no time by a fellow called Josh, who immediately wanted to go to your heroine's hotel room.

He was a skinny guy and in no way one of those beloved Suzy Size hunks like Troy, M. Idris or Beauregard. Suzy told him politely that she was not interested in his massage offer.

Then Josh said that he was so hungry and your motherly heroine handed him 50 Pesos. This was the beginning of a beautiful friendship, even though quite one-sided. Josh appeared in the Ermita neighbourhood out of nowhere every day to beg for his daily allowance and Suzy always paid him off, but also asked him: "Josh, what will you do, when I am gone?"

There are so many poor people in the Philippines: out of a population of 88 million, one third lives beyond the poverty line. There were naked and half-naked children in Adriatico Street every day. They were taking a bath in a steady flow of water that came from an underground water pipe that had probably burst several years ago. They were brushing their teeth with that water and adults were filling their kettles.

When Suzy Size arrived at Rizal Park, she had seen so many symptomatic signs of misery, she was ready for a rest. She walked by the memorial for a murderer, a wild guy called Lapu Lapu who killed Magellan, the great discoverer.

This is a funny country, Suzy thought, when she was asked by a guy sitting on a bench: "Where did you buy your shoes?"

You must know, gay tourist, there is nothing special about the shoes of Suzy Size, bought at unpretentious Tesco Lotus in Pattaya South. They are no high heels, since Suzy always travels disguised as manly Fritzy Frizz.

With a very deep voice, Suzy Size answered this strange question with a blunt, "In Thailand."

"And where are you from?"

"Switzerland."

"From Basel?"

"Zurich."

"What a coincidence! My sister is a nurse and will soon start to work in Zurich."

Oh dear, that old trick again! If Suzy had shown the slightest interest, that guy would have tried to befriend Suzy Size, or rather Fritzy Frizz. He then would invite his new buddy Fritzy for some beers, but would certainly always be at the toilet when a new check arrived.

Then he would invite slightly drunk Fritzy over to his house to meet his lovely sister who would be quite young. Then he would leave the room for a while and that sister would suddenly start screaming like hell. Then the brother would return and the sister would tell him and the policeman (who had come out of nowhere) that Fritzy had tried to rape her.

This one would have been a more expensive Philippine friendship than the one with poor Josh. Suzy Size left Rizal Park in a hurry.

GAY MANILA DAYS II
A nurse called Carlos

Suzy Size had to check her emails in Manila and thus entered an internet café in Adriatico Street. From the outside, she realised that this was a gay breeding ground.

Rainbow Pacific Suites has an inexpensive internet café downstairs and hotel rooms upstairs. The building is only a few years old and has an elevator. This is the only openly gay-owned and managed hotel in

Manila, maybe even the Philippines, which is a devout Catholic country and grossly overpopulated and poor.

Homosexuality (or bisexuality) is rampant, because all those young and always horny guys have no access to girls outside of marriage.

After Suzy Size paid for her internet session (they never write down the time when you start and always undercharge you), a receptionist called Marco showed Suzy a room.

They are spacious, have a view of Manila bay and all the amenities you need. The price of about US$36 is reasonable. The finishing of the room is quite lousy and can never compare to the standards in Thailand. The service does not match Thai standards either, one cannot but help get the impression they are all a bit on the dumb side and extremely slow here. But that seems to be a country-specific impression. They are not really mean, just a bit slow.

On the way down in the elevator, receptionist Marco — by asking the usual questions — had discovered that Fritzy Frizz was really a disguise of Suzy Size. He offered to visit your heroine, who had not yet moved to Rainbow Pacific Suites then, in her hotel. Suzy politely declined.

After she had moved into said hotel, Marco called her several times on the room phone and offered a 'visit'. So did Ian, another receptionist and a really ugly guy, who would not even have qualified if Suzy had been alone on a deserted island with him. Suzy is sure she could have had any of those guys working in that hotel and this spoilt it completely.

Their approaches all were so blunt, so unrefined, typical of males in a poor country who have problems getting laid. Therefore they are constantly horny.

Of Superman and Less Superb Men

When Suzy was young, she liked to go to the Philippines, because sex was so widely available, even in the most remote hamlets. But after more than 30-odd years of practice, it is more quality than quantity that your benign heroine is after.

Suzy Size selected Top and Bottom to be her headquarters in Manila. They have a nice outside terrace where you can see gay Manila pass by. (Inside they have one of those loud discos.)

Their waiters are well selected and cute or even sexy. Suzy fancied one, but his eyes so obviously followed the girls, Suzy made no effort to befriend him — which means, try to drag him into her bed. She is certain she could have achieved it with money in that poor country, but found it to be too dirty.

In Top and Bottom customers have to sign each and every order, so the drunks and cheats cannot deny the amounts they ordered. There are many street hustlers opposite Top and Bottom and they will — be warned gay tourist — always try to make eye contact or follow you when you walk away, making the usual blunt offers.

A rather cute guy sitting at the next table started a conversation with good old Suzy. His name was Carlos, and he was studying to become a nurse. That is almost the only way out of the misery in the Philippines, to become a nurse and go abroad.

Carlos was very pleasant and Suzy chatted with him all night. She then took him to BED (a gay disco, that is) where they had the 'Hot Hunk of the Year' contest that night. Nice event, but once you have seen a few of them, you will start yawning.

Then Suzy took Carlos to a popular local disco nearby where the music was incredibly loud, and air conditioning was nonexistent. When they finally left the place, they had to show a receipt to the guard downstairs, otherwise they would not have been allowed out. And if there ever should be a fire — fires are very frequent in the Philippines — nobody would get out of this trap alive.

Suzy did not want to invite Carlos to join her that night, but took his number and promised to call him the next day, which was a Sunday. But, such is life, your heroine did not feel like it the next day and also the subsequent few days. And that was probably a good idea.

She will always remember this friendly and funny guy in a positive way, not being disappointed by him like by most of the other Filipinos.

GAY MANILA DAYS III
A farting father of four

Suzy Size still can be naïve. When she met Antony, a student of economics at Sonata, one of the Manila bars, she thought she had found a real interesting friend. He seemed intelligent and informed, watching Bloomberg and reading the *Economist*. After a beer, they went to Rainbow Pacific Suites.

The sex was short and disappointing, but Suzy was presented a bill of 1,000 Pesos. Suzy would have never thought Antony to be a CB, a Call Boy. The disappointment was not about money, but about a severe lack of judgment on the part of your heroine.

What do you do in Manila during the days? Suzy Size roamed the streets noting the oddities of the place.

Not far from her hotel, in the middle of Ermita, they have live goats for sale. Everywhere, they offer instant photos for the so-called Rush IDs. Why is there such a sudden rush in rather slow-moving Manila?

Suspicious-looking Viagra and Cialis packages are offered by almost every street vendor. If you decline, they will offer you the company of a nice young lady.

Once, unnerved Suzy responded to an older man: "Go see that girl yourself." And he responded: "Oh, you are very friendly, very smart."

Suzy was a bit sorry to have lost her cool with that poor guy trying desperately to make a living. But at the next corner another one of the buggers offered those old coins (that are not very old) for sale again.

They call Suzy "Boss", "Sir", "Friend" and "Hey Joe". Signs advertise vacancies for 'Male Bed Spacer' — sounds a bit like Charles Dickens' time!

Out of boredom Suzy decided to take a ride on the local Skytrain, to see beautiful Blumentritt (flower step). When the train arrived, Suzy tried to enter the first car of Line 1, which was not as crowded as the others, but was sternly denied entry by a uniformed female train attendant.

Suzy missed that train and moved to the so called 'Male Area', which sounds nice, but it is not at all, and instead rather smelly. She started to understand the train attendant's actions. On Line 1, the first car is reserved for women and the elderly. The Filipinas are apparently constantly molested by their male counterparts.

When Suzy Size arrived in supposedly beautiful Blumentritt, she realised this was just another ugly Manila slum. Garbage everywhere, decay, destitute people sleeping somewhere on the streets.

Some guys were playing a game in the filthy Blumentritt roads, but interrupted their very important daily workload to ask your heroine: "Do you want to boom boom?" Of course, they were not offering themselves, but their sisters, wives or daughters.

Suzy met yet another Tony somewhere on the streets and invited him for a beer. He was from Cavite, a place outside Manila, 31 years old and a father of four. His wife knows about him boom booming with the guys and she is — pragmatically — not against this, as long the objects of desire are men and not girls. Suzy liked his honesty and took him to her hotel.

In front of the Rainbow Pacific Suites another guy approached them, offering to take part in a threesome. Suzy declined politely.

The sex with Tony was so-so, at least not as bad as with Antony, the future economist and present CB. And of course Suzy handed over the usual 1,000 Pesos.

When they were waiting for the elevator, Tony farted incredibly loudly, at the very moment it arrived. When they entered the lift, the stink was brought in by Tony — it was horrible!

A farting father of four, engaging in gay sex with some dubious Farang. Are there any role models left in this devout catholic country?

Suzy's time with 31-year-old Edwin was probably the nicest encounter with any Filipino on that trip. He is a typical Suzy Size hunk. She met him at Che Lu and did not have to be convinced to take him back with her.

He was able to give quite a good massage and perform a decent sex job, he seemed to have fun as well. Suzy wrote down his number, but he came back two days later on his own. The poor guy had gotten into a hold-up when riding a Cheepney home. They had stolen his mobile at gun point and he was therefore afraid that Suzy Size might want to see him again, but could not reach him on his old number.

The strangest encounter during those very strange Manila days happened in the toilet at Pacific Rainbow Suites. Suzy had just entered her hotel from outside and was too lazy to go up to her room for a pee, deciding to use the toilet downstairs instead.

When she walked in, a guy walked out, staring at your heroine. When she came out, he was still there waiting for Suzy.

"I am Joseph. I can give you a blowjob. Very cheap. Only 500 Pesos. You can fuck me." Suzy Size really had no such inclinations, but took the outspoken 34-year-old over to Jail Bar for some beers.

Jail is a nice beer bar. One of the gay waiters showed Suzy a short gay porn movie on his phone, he was so proud to have such bold stuff on his beloved mobile.

Joseph was a bit strange, but at least not boring. His customers in America send him US$50 through Western Union and he gets fucked for that amount, live in a hotel where they have webcams, the customer watching the act.

Oh precious internet, what the hell would we do without you?

IN SEARCH OF '101'
A phallic landmark in straight and gay Taipei

What a relief, to come from the messy, poor and pathetic Philippines, to an orderly and civilised country like Taiwan and its well-organised capital, Taipei. The immigration service at the ugly but functional airport is efficient and no-nonsense.

The taxi brought Suzy Size to her hotel in the centre of town for 1,000 Taiwan dollars (NT$) (about US$35), the reception had received the reservation, of course, and was incredibly friendly and forthcoming. In no time your heroine had checked in — travelling as Fritzy Frizz — and was led into a perfectly-fitted and designed room with all the amenities.

Of course there was air conditioning, TV, a safe in the room, as well as a brush for one's shoes and a shoe horn, etc. At NT$2,400, it was certainly not overpriced. The shower had a strong and steady flow as can be expected of Grohe fittings made in Germany, not like the trickle at Rainbow Pacific Suites in Manila.

Suzy went on one of her legendary walks the first thing after arriving. She soon found the main train station, where a young designer sold her some postcards he had created. He was a cute little guy, so Suzy could not resist and bought some, even though she has not sent postcards for at least two decades.

The last time your heroine visited Taipei was about 25 years ago. She had bought a ticket around the world, with a one-week stopover in Taipei. Suzy stopped over, but was a poor girl — a student — then, and could only afford to stay at a love hotel near that Taipei railway station. Suzy could not find that place now, but it was nearby. Astonishing what kind of memories still remain after such a long time.

Back then, nobody spoke English and Suzy had big problems communicating, your heroine was completely isolated during that week and no gay (or any other) encounter took place.

This time around, so many people in Taipei spoke English, it was easy to communicate. And all were incredibly friendly, the most friendly Chinese Suzy Size had ever met.

Suzy had heard about this giant phallic landmark building in Taipei called '101'. Far, far away from the railway station, Suzy could see it and was naturally interested to inspect that huge thing closely. She walked in that general direction, it took quite a while.

There are many well-groomed dogs to be seen on the streets of Taipei, some proud owners walk them on a leash, others tie them in front of their buildings. These dogs seem to be status symbols, like Mercedes cars elsewhere.

Taipei — unlike hellish Manila — is a very safe place, you can walk everywhere at any time. There are many police stations visible in Taipei, but none of those useless guards in Manila.

After maybe three hours of walking, Suzy arrived at '101', exhausted but proud. To enter it you have to go to the fifth floor and buy a ticket for NT$400. Suzy had to deposit her backpack in a locker and got in line, where she was asked by a guard, "Are you chewing gum?"

The tone left no doubt that this was a very, very dirty thing to do and Suzy Size felt caught in the act. She disposed of this filthy gum of hers in a garbage bin — after wrapping it neatly in a piece of paper — and thus returned to the civilised world and went up to the tower

The view was splendid and the architecture of the building modern Chinese. Taipei is not a very beautiful city, but not very ugly either. Comparably, Taipei is one of the smallest Asian capitals, with an unobtrusive, laid-back atmosphere.

It didn't take the seasoned eyes of your heroine very long to spot a young gay Chinese couple up on '101'. They were so sweet with each other and blended in very well with the rest of the visitors; Taiwan has very progressive gay rights laws.

Hopefully the civil achievements will survive closer ties with big China and an eventual reunification — which seems to be inevitable in the long term.

Suzy now needed a bite and a beer and entered one of the simple Chinese restaurants nearby in an older shop house area. She ordered a delicious noodle dish with seafood and an equally delicious Taiwan beer from the friendly owner who spoke English very well.

The man was a Vietnamese Chinese and his brother had fled Vietnam for Taiwan in 1975, together with other refugee boat people. The horrendous red tape took ten years to overcome, until he could finally join his brother in Taiwan in 1985. He married a Taiwanese woman and has two kids. Their daughter is studying in the US, whereas the younger son had a tutor over that evening.

While Suzy enjoyed her delicious Chinese noodle dish, they had ordered a pizza from Pizza Hut as a Saturday evening treat and drank Pepsi with it. They even offered Suzy a slice, but your heroine gratefully declined the nice offer. After that entire history lesson, Suzy was shifting into 'meat gear'.

She did not choose to go to gay Taipei 'Hans' sauna, even though she likes the name a lot. Suzy opted for Rainbow sauna, which was easily found.

But due to very bad karma or only old age, nobody there showed much desire to show Suzy Size the way to heaven. She watched a gay Chinese hunk get a blowjob from a Farang kneeling in front of him in a dark room. Another one was licking his tits. Suzy fumbled his ass a bit and helped herself jerk off. But the whole encounter was not too inspiring.

Later that night, Suzy Size also visited Funky. It is a smoky disco located in a cellar. A nice young crowd comes here during the weekend, it was very crowded that Saturday night. The guys were friendly and polite to your grey heroine, as can be expected in extremely friendly Taiwan, but of course no one showed any interest in Suzy. After the two beers she went back to her hotel and right to bed.

Your heroine was going to need all her power the next day, when she was visiting the 'So Young Men Spa'.

THE VERY BEST MASSAGE... EVER
An old queen is turned into a king

If you are looking for the very best of gay Taiwan, you naturally have to look in its capital, Taipei. Most major gay places are located within walking distance from Ximen MRT station and can be found easily.

Just opposite of Ximen station you will see an interesting building called Red Theatre Plaza. Behind it there is a two-storey building which houses dozens of gay bars, many with seats al fresco; a pure breeding ground of homosexuality.

Suzy had an iced coffee with a funny pink straw that slow Sunday afternoon, intently observing the square outside with all those tables and chairs under umbrellas.

It was a relaxed atmosphere; for the other guests, mainly groups of two to four or even five people, there was nothing much to do than talk the time away over a coffee.

Suzy stared at some of the other males congregating here, but understandably, no one showed any obvious interest in your hardened heroine. She read the most recent issue of the *Economist*.

How very normal homosexuality was here in Taipei. No need to be super flamboyant, eccentric or shrill. But then hedonist Suzy — from a different generation than these young and relaxed monogamous kids — was seriously thinking about a real gay (polygamous) Taipei encounter, and left.

She had discovered 'So Young Men Spa', was fascinated by the name and curiously visited their website. A muscular guy could be seen serving something on a tray to a customer reading a magazine in a waiting room; it was an intriguing photo.

After a short walk, Suzy Size found the building that houses 'So Young Men Spa' and went up to the reception. Your heroine was asked if she had made an appointment. Carelessly, she had not. She was seated in that very waiting room she recognised from the internet and handed a menu.

She chose a 'dessert' for NT$2,300 (about US$70) but was never given an album showing the 11 therapists who work at 'So Young Men Spa'. Not knowing who would take care of your heroine intensified the unique experience that was to come.

After maybe 5 minutes — another client had just left — a polished young man with glasses introduced himself as Gordon and led Suzy to the private massage room with en suite bathroom.

According to the spa's website (which does not show the masseurs), Gordon is 1.80 metres tall at 75kg, and 30 years young. Gordon, who with his glasses resembles Clark Kent quite a bit, could speak English fairly well.

Suzy lay down on her stomach, with her head in a hole on the table. She could not see a thing when Gordon started his great work, but had noticed that he had taken off his shirt and the glasses. Clark Kent thus was truly transformed into Superman. Suzy just let him do whatever he wanted with his magical hands that were touching your heroine everywhere.

The following two hours were pure pleasure, at one point Suzy laid on her back but was blindfolded by some sort of mask when Gordon was working on her face, just fantastic. Near the end he took off his clothes entirely and Suzy Size, after prolonged pleasures of the flesh, went right up to paradise.

This was the best and most erotic massage of her entire life, Suzy thought.

After a shower and getting dressed, Suzy was once again seated in that friendly waiting room. What would come next?

After a little while Gordon, properly dressed, and with his Clark Kent glasses back in place, served her a jelly plus a fruit salad and tea on a tray.

Suzy had ordered dessert from the menu and here it was indeed.

JUS PRIMAE NOCTIS
The strange straight ways back in Hong Kong

Your benign heroine learnt another lesson in Taiwan perfectionism when Suzy Size checked out of her impeccable Dong Wu Hotel.

The receptionist volunteered to come outside the hotel and flag down a taxi to the airport. Suzy declined the offer at first, but the friendly woman insisted.

When the taxi driver pushed a button from his seat to open the trunk for Suzy's small and compact suitcase, the woman yelled at him in Chinese and he immediately jumped out of the car to help your frail heroine with that small piece of luggage, and lifted it into the trunk.

"How rude!" the friendly receptionist woman muttered to puzzled Suzy.

The fare was once again agreed to be the usual NT$1,000 and about an hour later, Suzy approached the airport.

The driver took a wrong turn near departures and had to backtrack, apologising profusely to Suzy who could not care less with the fixed fare, but the man had obviously learnt his lesson from that wonderful receptionist.

But queuing up at the Philippine Airlines counter with all those ugly and overweight Filipino workers and all the Filipina maids on their mobile phones, Suzy had definitely left sophisticated Taiwan and returned to congested and unrefined Manila (or the Philippines in general).

The many talkative announcements — before take-off and during the entire flight — were as if they were addressing an especially slow and childish crowd. Besides being told to switch off the mobile phones about seven times, the passengers were ordered "not to congregate in any parts of the airplane, especially near toilets". Suzy — who in the early years of her gay life did sometimes congregate near or in toilets — had no such desires this time around.

The food was horrible, but the flow of wine plentiful and thus Suzy survived that awful flight and the imbecile crowd.

Your heroine had to change planes to Hong Kong in Manila. The heat in the bus to the terminal was horrible and Suzy thought, "Typical of the Philippines: First they shoot Benigno Aquino at this airport. Then they feel slightly sorry and name it after him."

Certainly rather incorrect thoughts, but Suzy had just returned from a civilised country to the Wild East and was suffering from acute culture shock.

Suzy had to go through the heavy security again — belt off, shoes off — well, maybe this was for the best, in a country as mad as the Philippines.

When Suzy was back in the plane (after another ride in a hot bus), the young girl beside her cried and prayed silently, moving her lips without a sound. Suzy was a bit puzzled, but also slightly moved.

This young Filipina closed her eyes again while praying and then drew a cross on her face and across her breast. She did that several times and only became a bit more relaxed when the plane was well on its way to her destiny.

Praying is a favourite pastime in the Philippines (besides banging). They had prayer sessions for Cory Aquino who got colon cancer while

Suzy was in the country. This is probably as successful as those prayers performed in the US by silly religious folks who ask God for a lower oil price right at the filling stations.

Cory Aquino has died in the meantime, naturally, but that may not convince devout Catholics of the futility of prayers. It may have helped to get her son elected president, but there is no solid proof of such.

The girl beside Suzy obviously believed in those ancient rituals. Fine. She was to become a domestic helper in Hong Kong, leaving her native Mindanao for the very first time.

Of course, she was not told about those rumoured strange straight rites in Hong Kong, also known as *jus primae noctis*. It allows the employers to have sex with those girls on the first night they arrive and sleep with them after. That young and innocent girl might have sensed something like that.

Your slightly moved heroine did not try to convert that devoted catholic girl to voodoo, which makes far more sense to Suzy Size (especially in such a dreadful situation) than Catholicism. She even went so far as to lie and tell the girl in the sweetest possible voice: "Everything will be all right, dear." But, of course, it was not going to be all right at all, dear!

After two more days in Hong Kong Suzy returned to Thailand via Macau, squeezing in some Portuguese mussels in Taipa and a Macau beer on a short stopover that only lasted a few hours.

Back in good old Pattaya, she did not think about the sad fate of that poor, naive Filipina in Hong Kong again. After all, you have to get life's priorities right: gay life must go on.

EXTRAS
Thailand

05

EXTRAS

It is still incredible how cheaply one can live in Pattaya. And there are always inexpensive extras within reach.

Porn DVDs in Jomtien beach for 80 Baht. Or if you are more into the arts — Suzy Size likes both spectrums of human nature — you can buy Hollywood movies for 100 Baht. Suzy got *Inglorious Basterds* by Quentin Tarantino. She was really looking forward to seeing Christoph Waltz, who won an Oscar for best performance as an actor in a supporting role.

When he won his award, Suzy read everywhere that Waltz was a "completely unknown actor". But that is not true; Suzy Size has known him for years. She has actually performed beside him on stage.

It must have been about 1984 or 1985 when *Amadeus* by Peter Schaffer was staged at Schauspielhaus in Zurich. A very young Christoph Waltz was Wolfgang Amadeus Mozart and Suzy stood by his side. She was an extra.

With fondness does your greying heroine think back on her seven years as an extra in Zurich. She was young, so young then and most other extras were young, too; gay and eager to play on and off stage. Suzy had most of them without any money involved, a very happy time without much fear of AIDS yet.

An extra plays a small, but important role. As a servant he delivers the so important message that keeps the action alive. If that darn message does not arrive, the play cannot go on.

How do you play a king? Or, should we say, a queen? You cannot. It is the surrounding that establishes a king on stage. If nobody bows, how can the audience know that the jerk over there is supposed to be a king?

Many Farangs seem to suffer from a lack of attention. To counter that terrible feeling (of neglect by the world), they group some money boys around themselves in Jomtien beach. The staff, those paid boys, will listen to what that eloquent Farang has to say in carefully chosen English terms. He is here on a mission. He will explain everything. But few of these Farangs realise that those simple Thai boys do not understand even a quarter of what they say.

Suzy Size, working restlessly in her garden, suffers from attention syndrome too, at times. The cows nearby do not take much notice of your heroine, nor do they seem to sense how wise she is.

Move to Pattaya, gents, if you suffer from that feeling. There are still some (extra) empty beach chairs in Jomtien. And you can buy all the extras you need for a little money.

They will certainly pretend to listen, but will understand little. And this is perhaps better for all parties involved.

IN INDIA, NOTHING IS WHAT IT SEEMS
India

06

DO ALL THE (HORNY) GAY MUMBAI MEN MEET AT HORNIMAN CIRCLE?

As a first time visitor to India, Suzy Size worried about lots of things when leaving Castelgandolfo in the early hours of the morning.

In one hour and ten minutes, your heroine reached Bangkok airport, with Khun Amorn driving as usual. When the straight Swiss couple travelling with Suzy arrived as well, they checked in.

The inexpensive four-and-a-half-hour Jet Airways flight left on time and was perfect, but the landing in Mumbai was delayed by an hour due to traffic congestion. The customs formality in incredible India took no time at all and — after changing some US Dollars into Rupees — the trio stood in front of their small prepaid cab that ran on liquid gas.

But where to store the extensive luggage containing all the numerous frocks, high heels and fur coats of your heroine? The tank for the liquid gas had taken up the limited space in the trunk.

The driver put all the stuff on the roof, secured it with a rope — apparently an old Indian rope trick — and an hour later they arrived at Hotel Manama (booked through the Internet), centrally located around the corner of Mumbai main station, also known as Victoria Station.

Well, this Hotel Manama was a horrible dump and completely run-down. The staff was unfriendly and, if they had developed any expertise over the long years of their existence, it was in the field of non-service. The price of about US$35 is a very bad joke for that small, dirty room in that noisy hotel, the bed sheets being of very dubious cleanliness.

The three travellers decided to stay for one night only and immediately went on a walk toward the nearby Mumbai Colaba tourist area in search of a better hotel.

First-time visitor Suzy was overwhelmed by the constant noise and masses of people in the streets, the horrible and constantly honking cars and that incredible traffic and air pollution.

Suzy passed Horniman Circle Gardens and was intrigued by the interesting name: is it here that all the horny Indian hunks meet at night? She has since checked it out, but must report the disappointing news — she could not find any of those expected horny men there and the name is definitely misleading. Suzy Size drew her first conclusion on this latest trip: apparently, in India nothing is what it seems.

Mumbai was still suffering from the trauma caused by the November terrorist attacks that had happened shortly before Suzy's visit. She saw road blocks all over and many policemen guarding the central area, which was so unsafe during the prolonged siege in the heart of Mumbai. The state police headquarters is located just three minutes away from the Taj Mahal Hotel and they were really shown to the whole world as a bunch of completely incompetent idiots.

But now normalcy had returned. In the evening, your heroine saw masses of people gathering once again in front of the Taj Mahal Hotel and the Gateway of India. It is a popular pastime to sit, stand and stroll in the area enjoying the cooler hours of the day. And exactly here — gay tourist to India — there is cruising going on. But your heroine, still looking for a more suitable hotel, had no time for hanky panky at the moment.

Suzy Size had heard all these stories about food poisoning, dysentery, cholera, all those horror stories about India — you have probably heard of them too. But walking by the Leopold Café and Bar (in the heart of Colaba) where practically all the seats were taken by Farangs and locals, where they serve those huge pitchers of beer, and the menu is extensive and the food looks tasty, your heroine — quite hungry by now — decided to risk her life and have a bite.

After all, the Leopold has existed since 1871 and can therefore not have poisoned *all* its customers. And really, it was quite good, and the beer in particular restored the low spirits of your heroine to more acceptable levels.

Near the Leopold, Suzy found a suitable hotel named the Cowies Hotel. Suzy and company booked rooms for the next day and stayed there during all their memorable Mumbai days.

While walking back to her horrible hotel that very first night, Suzy Size saw many strange signs: "No postings!" just beside some postings, which were at least not covering the "No postings!" warning. "Hope: The Nursing Home", and "Strictly no parking in front of this gate. Tires will be deflated." But the tires of the car parked directly in front of that gate were not deflated.

But the most worrisome signs all over Mumbai were the ones for all those clinics treating STDs (sexually transmitted diseases). Back in comfortable Pattaya, you cannot possibly imagine how many of them are displayed in Mumbai!

Suzy Size had a hard time sleeping the first night, all those STD signs reoccurring in her nightmarish dreams, chasing away any sound sleep like nasty ghosts. Only later did your frightened heroine learn what STD really stands for in Mumbai: State Telephone Dialing.

Apparently, nothing in India is really what it seems.

THE ONLY GAY BAR BETWEEN ISTANBUL AND BANGKOK FINALLY FOUND!
A trip to Elephanta where the lingam is still revered

Suzy Size — together with Sahib and Mam, the straight couple who constituted your heroine's entourage — booked a city tour in front of Cowies Hotel. A driver with a small air-conditioned taxi drove them around this mega-city with 20 or more million inhabitants. The price at US$12 seemed reasonable and that little excursion was very useful to see the sights of Mumbai, which most people still call Bombay.

The trio visited Marine Drive, a fancy and expensive area where celebrities live. This was followed by Jaine Temple, the first of so many Hindu temples in India where a sign clearly stated: "Ladies in monthly period are not allowed." Well, Miss Size (or rather Fritzy Frizz) could enter without any problem.

Then a visit to Malabar Hill in the uptown rich residential area. The driver parked outside the Hanging Garden, also known as Phirojshah Metha Garden — it was nothing special.

When they drove down the hill the taxi had to stop in front of a red light, and that is when those begging children became a real nuisance for the first time. They molested the three Farangs through the open window, poor little creatures, but their smell — aside from their constant begging — was so unbearable, the windows were finally closed.

It took a while before the real culprit of this intensive foul odour was discovered: it was your unlucky heroine. When she had re-boarded the taxi at the Hanging Garden, it was parked beside a wall. And Suzy Size did not see that big piece of shit she stepped into. Her whole shoe was covered and parts of that stinking mass even entered it and smeared her precious, pretty foot.

At the next stop — the 'Washing Laundry', which is the biggest open-air laundry place in the world — your blushing and highly embarrassed heroine cleaned herself and her shoe (a lot of perfume was used, too).

With great interest Suzy Size looked out of her window in Parkland Road, which is also known as 'Fuckland Road': it is the red light district of Mumbai where countless women offer their services to the not very discerning customers. According to the taxi driver, a short time costs 200 Rupees (about US$4), but Suzy Size did not try to verify this.

Of course the Mahatma Gandhi Museum was visited as well, he was a virtuous man certainly, but Suzy Size has a different, less virtuous concept of life. She could never live without her beautiful frocks, her expensive jewels, her many high heels and her beloved boys.

Cruising is extremely difficult in Mumbai. There is some cruising going on, on the beach promenade in front of the Taj Mahal Hotel. But the longer you are in Mumbai, the less you try to meet anyone's eye. As soon as you establish eye contact, the good-looking (or not so good-looking) guy will try to sell you some junk instead of his meat.

You will certainly meet a young man here that wants to sell you one of those gigantic and certainly phallic balloons, at a "very good price". But you would really like to buy a piece of his ass, if anything at all.

Or someone will try to sell you an 'Indian Air Conditioner'. This is an ordinary fan made of peacock feathers. But — if you wanted anything from him at all — you might just want to suck him. Or you may be offered a shoe shine that could be the shoe shine of your life! But you really just want a so-called massage from this beautiful boy.

Suzy bought a ticket to Elephanta Island from a very ugly man. The ride to the island takes about an hour and costs 120 Rupees (US$2.40). But as soon as you enter the boat and start to climb up to the upper deck, you are charged another 10 Rupees for that privilege. 10 Rupees is very little money, but Suzy Size watched herself getting angry and shouting at that jerk.

You are constantly harassed in Mumbai by these destitute people that want to sell you useless stuff, beg outright or charge you for something you think you should not be charged for. They finally drag you down to their level and you start to fight with them over the ridiculous amount of 10 Rupees (20 cents).

There was a sexy young man on the boat; the first guy in India Suzy Size really wanted to have. But he was a vendor, who tried to sell her postcards and brochures, then some cheap and absolutely useless necklaces, then a third kind of junk, so Suzy just watched (and lusted after) him from the corner of her eyes. Just no eye contact!

The caves of Elephanta are very interesting. They are a World Heritage Site and very old. Over the years, countless columns, reliefs and lovely lingams were carved out of the stones, a hell of a job. Suzy Size admired them all and is glad she took that ride over to Elephanta.

But it was now time to return to Mumbai and have a look at the only gay bar between Istanbul and Bangkok. It is only gay on Saturday nights and today was Saturday, your heroine's last night in Mumbai. By chance it was her birthday, too.

But first Suzy Size had to find the place. She had no address, only a name: Vodoo. Suzy knew it was somewhere in her neighbourhood in the Colaba area and asked for directions. It was only a five-minute walk from her hotel and when she arrived that Saturday evening, she immediately had an interesting encounter with 26-year-old Ashok.

EXPERIENCE THE ONLY MUMBAI GAY BAR
Ashok and Raj: two Mumbai men

When Suzy Size was looking for Vodoo — supposedly the only gay bar between Istanbul and Bangkok — she did not immediately see the sign in that sea of signs. When she walked up and down the road, she was approached by a young man who had sensed that she was looking for something in that entertainment area.

When your restless heroine asked him about Vodoo, he knew it instantly and pointed at the place just a few metres back. And then he offered to give a massage. Of course, he knew of a little inexpensive hotel nearby.

Ashok was 26 years old, pleasant and not bad looking, but with that somewhat ridiculous moustache that is so common in India. He just was not quite the type of man Suzy likes, she hates moustaches. The friendly offer was therefore declined.

It was about 8pm and Ashok told Suzy that it was useless to go to Vodoo before 9.30pm when it opens. He knew of a bar nearby that served beer for only 100 Rupees (US$2) and was willing to be taken there for some cold drinks that would also pass the time. Well, Suzy is easily lured by the prospect of a cold beer and followed her newest friend Ashok to that nearby joint without any delay.

There Mr. Ashok told Suzy about his life in a nutshell: he was born in some hamlet in the Indian countryside and had — thanks to a scholarship — studied history in Mumbai. He then worked as a journalist for a while, which is a dangerous profession in a country where the mighty are so ruthless. He stopped doing that dangerous work and turned to his present (and comparably harmless) profession as a male-male masseur.

Hanging around Vodoo and in front of the nearby Taj Mahal Hotel, he made a living. He showed Suzy the names and telephone numbers of his Farang acquaintances in a little booklet. For a discounted 1,000 Rupees (US$20) he would do his job. He advertised his massage skills in the bar again and again and did not forget to mention that he had a big cock. He was a top and always used condoms. Since Suzy is a top as well, there was no convergence in sight. But Ashok had the idea to hire a girl that they both could fuck, an offer your blushing heroine declined as well.

After two beers and a nice tip Suzy Size parted ways with Ashok and returned to Vodoo. It was now 10pm and the time ripe to finally discover gay Mumbai. The entrance fee at Vodoo on Saturdays is 350 Rupees (US$7.50) and does not include any drinks at all. A little bottle of beer is 150 Rupees (US$3).

As Ashok had predicted, female guests made up about 70% of the crowd at this early stage of the evening. Suzy Size sat at the bar and looked around. Not far from her was a rather good-looking young man, who reminded your heroine a bit of the French actor Alain Delon when he was young — this one here was thinner though. He did not react to the scanning eyes of Suzy Size.

There were some tables in the back where the women were sitting. One of them approached Suzy and asked for a drink. Suzy explained that she only liked boys and therefore saw no need to buy her a drink. She left Suzy, obviously surprised by her un-Indian frankness.

Suzy ordered another beer for herself — what a way to spend a birthday! Exactly a year ago Suzy had been in Jakarta, that horrible capital of Indonesia. But you may say anything bad about Jakarta, at least they have that civilised gay massage place called 9M in unforgettable Jalan Talang Betutu, where your heroine had a birthday boy last year.

As the night wore on, the more guests arrived at Vodoo. There were more men here now and the female hustlers were in the minority. There were some obvious money boys and some well-off Indians: they could have been fashion designers or similarly fancy professionals. Some Farangs were there too. They were dancing those Indian group dances from those Bollywood movies, but all the men were obviously gay. Suzy had fun just watching them.

The Indian version of Alain Delon had finally signalled interest in

Suzy and your heroine tried to start a conversation with him. But his English was so basic, Suzy only found out his name, Raj, and his age, 24. A lack of conversation has never been an insurmountable obstacle when it comes to sex, but Suzy had just too much cash hidden in her room to take young Delon home. She signalled: no interest.

This provoked the whore that wanted a drink before to undertake a new attempt: she approached your heroine again with the same intention. Suzy declined. Then she offered and praised the thinner Delon (maybe her brother?): "He is a very nice boy."

She was willing to translate the conversation to keep the business going, but Suzy was not really interested. Delon left for the dark area near the toilet. When Suzy had a pee later, she saw him in conversation with some Indian ladyboys. They admired him for his youth and his male beauty, a role that the little macho obviously enjoyed.

It must be said, the toilet in Vodoo is a bit on the dirty side. Somebody had recently vomited and that well-known sourish smell was still in the air.

Delon, still being adored by the ladyboys when Suzy returned, had now become rather like a peacock. His manner reminded Suzy of some strange Italian money boys she met in the 1980s. They would allow their customers to blow their horn or would fuck them — but certainly no unmanly kissing. And after the action, they often would turn violent and ask for more or all money around, to restore their macho self-image.

Suzy Size watched the frantic dancing at Vodoo for a while, then returned to her hotel room alone. Better to be safe than sorry, especially on a birthday.

MORE (GAY) SEX IN THE INDIAN COUNTRYSIDE THAN IN CITIES

Before Suzy Size came to India, she was never interested in that overly huge country. She was just there because of her self-chosen mission (or fate) to describe the whole of Asia from a gay perspective.

The straight couple — Sahib and Mam (the word 'Mam' is pronounced like 'mad') — was going on a four-week tour of India, before finally attending in a wedding in Jaipur. That seemed like the perfect opportunity to get an impression of that unimaginable country.

After landing in Udaipur airport (the flight had taken 1 hour and 40 minutes), the three adventurers were picked up by their driver Mr. Kalyan, who — over the three-week tour — turned out to be an outstanding imitator of animal and bird voices. He could imitate no less than 175 animal voices and was presently learning another 50. His plan was to enter the Guinness Book of World Records and then perform on Indian TV shows and finally become rich. But for the time being, he was still a driver.

After Mumbai — without any sex — your heroine had high hopes for the countryside. Suzy had read in *DNA* (*Daily News Analysis*, a daily newspaper) that more people in the countryside have premarital sex (that seems to be sex in general) than in the cities. The main reason for that surprising finding is the lack of privacy in the highly overpopulated cities: they have no place to get laid.

And indeed, in Cowies Hotel, Suzy Size was surprised by how many people there were. Some in odd niches. In the corridors. In the elevator. Obscure backrooms. People, everywhere.

When checking out of that hotel, no less than six porters had 'helped' with the luggage. In other words, six people wanted a tip.

The first impression of Udaipur was great. The hotel was in the old part of the city and had a rooftop restaurant from where one could see the palace and the main Hindu temple, which was terribly loud in the early mornings.

Sahib and Mam hired a guide the next day to visit the old buildings. He was a fairly good-looking 27-year-old guy who spoke English and French, but was lost to mankind since his marriage about a year ago.

These Udaipur guys are (or were) warriors, and they all have moustaches, except when their father dies and they then shave them off in grief.

The palace of the Maharaja (or Maharani) of Udaipur is fantastic. Suzy Size, your restless heroine, was deeply impressed. Such riches, such incredible amounts of artifacts, marble stuff, weapons, jewellery... you would not believe it.

The favourite white horse of the Maharaja had been disguised as a baby elephant, with an artificial trunk added to its snout before an important battle with some long-forgotten mogul rulers. Did that travesty work? Suzy does not really know, but in her motherly ways, hopes so.

Walking through the crowded lanes of Udaipur, Suzy discovered Farang restaurants like Café Edelweiss, and many French and German bakers. She saw plenty of cows shitting all over, but the beasts were not bothered at all by the locals. On the contrary, the cows were revered, fed and milked, tons of grass being transported into all those cities in the half desert, in order to nourish the masses of holy cows.

And sexually speaking? Nobody was sexy, nobody seemed to know what a guy like your heroine might be interested in. Be warned, gay tourist to India, if you want to get laid in Udaipur, take a juicy Thai boy with you.

When Suzy Size went up to one of those many roof top restaurants overlooking the city, she ordered a Kingfisher beer.

You must know, there are basically two kinds of Kingfisher, the Lager and the Strong. Lager has about 5% alcohol, the Strong beer contains 8%, which knocks you out. In Udaipur she ordered a Lager.

The waiter explained that your heroine could certainly have a beer, but since they had no alcohol license and their Indian customers might object, it would be served in a tea pot. Suzy Size got her ice-cold Kingfisher in a teapot, which is not the worst way to drink beer — certainly better than no beer.

THE MAHARAJA OF DUNGARPUR'S MASSEUR
The strange rites of those notorious straights

Very few people make it to Dungarpur these days. International tourism to India was way down shortly after the terrorist attacks in Mumbai. And in Rajasthan there seem to have been other violent terrorist attacks in the past, with hundreds of deaths.

That straight couple — mainly Sahib, who had done the reading and planning, whereas Mam just followed and nagged — wanted to go to Dungarpur, where the Maharaja has turned his palace into a partial hotel with 23 rooms. And that suited Suzy Size just fine. You must know, gay India tourist, the Sizes have been friends with the Dungarpurian Maharajas for over a century. Or at least that is what your heroine, Miss Size, fantasised.

It took only about two and a half hours to reach Dungarpur from Udaipur. On the way, there were countless trucks bearing the sign 'Blow Horn'. And Suzy naturally thought of blowing horn all the time.

The Udai Bilas Palace of Dungarpur turned out to be most suitable and accommodating indeed. Situated in lush gardens — reminiscent of Castelgandolfo — it overlooked a little lake with hundreds of birds in a sanctuary.

Very few people were presently staying at Udai Bilas Palace (only 5 out of 23 rooms were occupied). Suzy Size was shown several rooms before she finally made her pick. There were no locks on the doors, since theft is completely unheard of in the Dungarpurian Palace. A spacious room, with fine furniture, a ceiling fan and also air conditioning available, all well established, old-fashioned, just beautiful.

But the most spacious part of Suzy Size's quarters was the bathroom with an old bathtub, tropical shower and toilet. There even was a desk in this cathedral of cleanliness and Suzy Size may as well have written this recent chapter in that very toilet. But first she had to take (if you excuse the blunt language) a dump, and — in retrospect — she must agree to probably having never defecated more regally anywhere else than in this grand toilet.

Before the midday heat got unbearable, Suzy and the straight couple visited the old palace of the Maharaja of Dungarpur up the hill.

It was a bit run-down, but alright. On one of the upper floors, behind a lockable iron door, were paintings of a special kind.

Dungarpur can be a bit boring at times, not unlike Jomtien beach, where you can buy some porn DVDs if you are too lazy for the real thing. Behind the iron door, the Maharaja had had scenes of the Kama Sutra painted, a fact that ignited the spirits of Sahib, who had been rather lethargic lately. He sucked in all those dirty scenes with his greedy eyes; any honorable homosexual would have been appalled.

In order to see that dirty stuff better, Sahib went on his knees in front of the Kama Sutra, as if he wanted to give it a blowjob. Whenever he took a picture of that obscene stuff, his perverse camera made a "wow" sound that he had apparently programmed in preparation for such embarrassing moments. Mam, his unamused wife, less blushing than your heroine, finally had to drag Sahib by his ears away from that revolting material.

Suzy strongly suspects that the old straight couple — when they finally returned to the privacy of their room — tore off their clothes and immediately tried the new positions they had learned that educational morning. Such are the strange rites of the notorious straights!

While walking through Dungarpur village, Suzy Size had discovered quite a handsome boy. But it was naturally out of question to ask him to visit your heroine at the palace.

First of all, his English was practically non-existent. Secondly, his father, who was a simple tailor, seemed to watch over the boy's future with great care and suspicion when he glanced at your heroine, who tried to look as harmless as she possibly could, disguised as friendly Fritzy Frizz. Thirdly, he was only a commoner, possibly from a low caste.

How could Lady Size have taken such a simple (but certainly juicy) man to the Palace of the Maharaja of Dungrapur without raising an eyebrow or two? What possible explanation could she offer the (disgruntled) Maharaja for the presence of that simple village boy? That she had ordered a wedding dress from the sweet boy's tailor father? Ha!

Suzy Size had a much better, more suitable and practical idea. She had made arrangements to meet the Maharaja of Dungarpur's masseur in the palace. The hour cost 650 Rupees (US$15) for a so-called 'scientific' massage, which sounded thrilling — or terrifying, if you prefer.

Before she had made the booking, Suzy had checked that they only had male masseurs for men at the palace. His age was supposed to be around 35 years; not too old, not too young for your heroine. Suzy took a foam bath in her room, sprinkled all kind of oriental perfumes and scents over her wornout body and met said masseur punctually at 3.45pm in the designated massage room. The door was closed and Suzy Size laid on the massage table, eager for the outcome of this new adventure.

To cut her endless waiting and this long story short: nothing happened at all. The massage was OK, but nothing of what you (and your heroine) were secretly hoping for. All those 'Blow Horn' signs in India do not really mean what they should.

India — where East meets West, and West meets East — is a very strange country indeed.

A FINAL FULFILLMENT — A NUCLEAR EXPLOSION? — IN THE DESERT NEAR JAISALMER
Gay life in India is complicated at times,
but green chocolate helps

Suzy Size was riding a camel in the desert near Jaisalmer. Your heroine was in high spirits. She had bought a very interesting chocolate at a dedicated Bhang shop in town, a chocolate which was all green and not the kind she normally gets in her home country, Switzerland. She had taken a large piece of that sweet stuff and was laughing non-stop on a camel named Lucky. An unbiased observer would probably say she was laughing like an idiot on that camel.

Her thoughts went back to the beautiful hotel attendant with a killer smile at the Imperial hotel of Jaisalmer. His name was Dipak, a sweet 22-year-old, just gorgeous.

Now, riding that camel through the desert under the influence of the magic chocolate, Suzy Size had a hard-on. Dull and difficult India was suddenly easy because of Dipak.

When Dipak had made the bed of your heroine in the morning, she had tipped him with 100 Rupees (about US$2), which is a high tip in India for such a simple clerk. The tips of their fingers had touched when the banknote was handed over and Dipak had smiled at Suzy — that knowing smile, gay tourist to India. This boy was clearly in the league of Troy, M. Idris or even Beauregard. Suzy was sure lovely Dipak would hang around near her room when she got back to the hotel and slip in when nobody else was looking.

But how the hell had Suzy Size gotten from Dungarpur to Jaisalmer?

Well, actually your heroine — travelling with that straight and ever-nagging couple Sahib and Mam — had visited Mount Abu first after Dungarpur (look the details up on a map, gay India tourist, if you are interested in such banal things as geography).

Mount Abu is a holy place with a stunning old marble temple where, for odd reasons, nobody may take any pictures. A sunset was consumed at Sunset Point, a sunset which was nothing special but, as the travellers were told, of great karmic value.

The trio then travelled to Ranakpur where another stunning temple had to be visited. Then their friendly driver — who fed the holy cows every morning with devotion — drove them safely to Jodhpur. In Jodhpur, your heroine got that peculiar India feeling for the very first time on that trip.

Admittedly, Suzy Size has never been to India before. What does she know about the subcontinent? Very little. As a child she had seen the movie *Around the World in 80 Days* with David Niven — probably her main source of information about India — and Jodhpur seemed like the ideal set for filming that old movie.

Incredible traffic, cows all over, smells from the open sewage system (but not as smelly as Bikaneer later in the trip, where the whole city smells like a gigantic shit hole), masses of people, many beggars, the mighty fort overlooking that messy and chaotic city; the mightiest fort so far.

Incredible riches were assembled in its palace, jewellery and fearsome arms of all kinds; those Maharajas really knew how to amass money and keep their subjects underfoot.

The three friends stayed at Suncity hotel, which was decent. They have a very wise policy at this particular hotel: "Lady guests of ill-repute are not allowed." But what about male guests? Well, they are really difficult to find in India, it seemed to Suzy.

In the evening, your heroine headed for the underground bar at Suncity hotel called Chahat ('Desire'). It is a bit dirty, rather run-down like most watering holes in India where drinking in general is not encouraged, and banned outright in many places.

Suzy ordered one of those strong Kingfisher beers with 8% alcohol content. At the neighbouring table were four younger guys who greeted your heroine. After a while one of them pitied Suzy who was sitting alone (but did not really feel lonely) and asked permission to join her.

He was 21, a student of the business administration trade. He asked Suzy what she was always asked in India: was she married? He could not understand that anybody at the tender age of your heroine could not be married. He himself was going to be married next year and invited Suzy to the occasion. Suzy said she would gladly attend (if she was around), but this really was a conventional lie.

Suzy is against marriage (straight or gay) because it is — like war — easy to get into, but difficult to get out of. Suzy had read that sentence somewhere recently.

He introduced his friends. One of them was not only good-looking, but also a fashion designer. As you must know, gay tourist, in India — as it is everywhere in the world — many fashion designers are gay.

Suzy Size had just read in one of those gossipy Indian newspapers about the sad plight of many male fashion models. Many of them are sexually molested by their fashion designers, who just tell them: "You know how it works." Meaning: either you perform privately with me, or you do not perform publicly for me.

It is now quite sure, almost certain: if Suzy Size had been born in India (which must have been prevented with excellent karma), she would have had no other choice than to become a fashion designer, even though she is nearly talent-free in this department.

So when that 21-year-old fashion designer came over to Suzy's table, your heroine expected highly interesting company. (By the way: It would have been easy to smuggle him past the reception. The elevator went down to this cellar bar and they could proceed to the privacy of Suzy Size's quarters in no time, without anybody knowing that your clever heroine had brought in a male of so called ill-repute.)

But, alas, that fashion designer was married. OK, it was a pre-arranged marriage when he was 8 years old and he had actually married her at 16 (she being 13 then). And he thought pre-arranged marriages were "unfair". But not out of desirable reasons.

He was just very polygamous, loved to fuck girls and boasted about all his many girlfriends. He boasted about his porn collection, too, with all those blond women with big tits, getting fucked and giving blowjobs to darker men (he described it vividly). Young men in India, Suzy realised, who visit bars and drink alcoholic beverages are vice-prone.

They like to have sex — like all young men — but probably do not get as much as they would like. The many girlfriends of the fashion designer became somewhat dubious. These were all just horny young men who would probably have sex with each other as well, if nobody knew about it and if they were a bit tipsy and had a place to go to. Try your luck, gay tourist to India, in that wonderful hotel and its basement 'Desire' bar, if you happen to pass through Jodhpur.

The next morning the three friends — Sahib, Mam and Suzy — continued their restless trip through Rajasthan. The half desert outside the window now resembled a full desert, but there were still lots of cows around. Huge trucks bring tons of grass to the desert city of Jaisalmer in order to feed all those animals.

Not far from Jaisalmer, Indian scientists have conducted nuclear explosions underground when they developed their atomic bomb. While Suzy was in India, they also tested a new rocket there.

The presence of the army in the area bordering Pakistan is very visible, after all this is the archenemy. You pass countless heavy army vehicles with lots of troops, canons and other mighty equipment.

On one occasion, when Sahib was asked the usual question by an Indian to start a conversation — what country he was from — he returned the question: "And you? Are you from Pakistan?"

"That is very unfriendly of you, Sir, I love my India!" Sahib's joke thus was not well received and he might have been punched on the nose.

One of the evening pastimes in Jaisalmer is to watch the sunset from a place where the nobility of that city is cremated. Again, it is good for karma. And here — at last — gay India was found!

Somebody had written on a wall: "Aman is gay." And this is finally proof that they must have heard about such things — even in the desert city of Jaisalmer.

Suzy Size (still under the influence of that magical and completely legal green chocolate) finally returned from her desert trip to the Imperial Hotel of Jaisalmer. Your heroine had high hopes to drag that wonderful Dipak — her one and only love beside Troy, M. Idris and Beauregard — into her room, into her bed and maybe even into her life.

But bloody, bloody India! The young man had the evening off and was not there at breakfast either.

JAIPUR – THE PINK CITY
Two men are banned from speaking to your heroine

Suzy Size — constantly in search of gay India which was so hard to discover — was not bored, had not yet suffered severe culture shock, but was also not too enthusiastic about that huge country and its strange inhabitants with their baffling beliefs.

Somewhere along the way they had visited Shiri Karni Mata temple, another beautiful marble temple, where rats are revered. Thousands of them are fed with milk each day. Suzy is no friend of rats and thinks it outright silly to feed and revere them.

To enter that strange temple, one could not wear any leather items such as belts or wallets and certainly no shoes. While Sahib and Mam had brought some socks, Suzy was walking through said temple barefoot. In other words, she was walking through all that rat shit without any shoes on, which was disgusting. Sahib and Mam threw their socks into the next garbage bin after that visit and Suzy washed her feet thoroughly and then sprayed them with alcohol.

Another odd place was the holy city of Pushkar, where a sign in the hotel informed the visitors that it was illegal to bring in alcoholic beverages. Suzy, who had a bottle of vodka in her suitcase, had therefore committed another criminal act.

In Pushkar they are hyper fundamental vegetarians; all meat is banned in the city, even eggs are illegal. Whenever silly laws are in place, there is a way out. Suzy Size naturally found a restaurant where they not only served beer, but also clandestinely offered those outlawed eggs. Your heroine went for the beer, but had no eggs, she had a plate of spaghetti instead to avoid another spinach with cottage cheese.

Believers in the Hindu faith wash off their sins in the highly polluted Pushkar Lake. Suzy Size — who is known to be a sinner — felt no urge at all to wash off any of hers with that dirty water. Suzy has always been agnostic, but had she not been before, she most certainly would have become one in Pushkar.

Tiger-watching was next on the program at Kanthambhore National Park. They had open jeeps for groups of 20 tourists. Early in the morning, the three friends were picked up at their hotel and driven around to other hotels until the vehicle was full.

Countless peacocks and birds were seen in that large nature reserve. Then a leopard was the first sensation. Some ordinary deer could be seen grazing — no big deal, they had seen many outside Jaisalmer, too.

And, yes, then your heroine was fortunate once again: an adult tiger could be observed from the safety of the car. He was maybe 70 metres away, probably bored by all those gazing tourists.

India is really a strange country. It is relatively easy to see a tiger in the wild, but it is extremely difficult to find that gay experience.

Suzy Size pinned all her fading hopes on the infamous Bouncer Bar in Jaipur, which is also known as Pink City. The reason for this interesting name is not what you might have suspected, gay tourist to India. It is named for the walled old town with an interesting bazaar which is entirely in pink.

After arriving in Jaipur, Suzy Size said goodbye to her two straight travel companions, who were attending a four-day Indian marriage.

Having checked into her hotel, Suzy wanted to go for a walk, but heavy rains started and at 2pm, the entire city was pitch dark. Suzy Size had never seen anything like this before. Where had the sun gone? Had the end of the world finally arrived?

Actually, a sandstorm had hit Jaipur together with that heavy downpour. When it finally stopped, Suzy took a taxi to a place near the walled city. And just by walking down an important-looking road, she bounced into Bouncer Bar.

How many times has the same thing happened to you, gay traveller? You walk around in a new city. You are more or less familiar with the names of the gay places, but have no clue where they actually are located. And then, unsuspectingly, you stand in front of said place!

Suzy Size entered Bouncer Bar. There was no electricity due to the storm, they had lit some candles. It was still very dark and your heroine almost fell down some stairs at the entrance.

Bouncer Bar occupies two floors, and it is quite run-down like the Maharaja hotel above. Suzy Size ordered a Kingfisher Lager. There were only men (as usual) in this Indian watering hole. Nobody was interested in this strange, foreign visitor.

A young boy — maybe 12 years of age — kneeled on the floor. With a bucket of water and a cleaning rag he tried to clean the floor by hand. He was very dirty himself and his cleaning efforts seemed more or less hopeless. He just was moving the dirt around, diluting it at best. It was a scene that could have come out of Oliver Twist.

Suzy Size paid her very cheap bill and tipped that friendly waiter most generously. When your heroine returned later for another look at this strange bar, the well-tipped waiter brought a Kingfisher Lager immediately without Suzy ordering it. Electricity had returned and the TV showed the usual Bollywood crap.

Amber Fort the next morning turned out to be the most majestic, most impressive of all those many historic buildings visited in all of Rajasthan. If you are lazy, you can ride an elephant up the hill, but your heroine preferred walking. What riches, what might Amber Fort represents! Two more forts were visited by your heroine in Jaipur, but she had now enough of all that cultural stuff. She returned to Bouncer Bar for a final visit.

The same waiter brought a Kingfisher Lager without Suzy asking for it. The TV showed Bollywood crap as usual. The Oliver Twist boy was there and tried his luck again with that bucket and the cleaning rag kneeling on the dirty floor. It was a hopeless, totally futile undertaking.

Then two guys asked permission to join your heroine at her table.

The older one said he was a doctor, but looked more like a hoodlum. The younger one was cute and Suzy Size would have loved to take him up to the shabby rooms of the Maharaja hotel. But then, the well-tipped waiter interfered and banned the two men from even talking to your heroine. They returned to their table and shortly afterwards left Bouncer Bar.

The interfering waiter probably knew something about that unequal pair that Suzy Size did not know and thus your half-baked heroine may have been prevented from being harmed.

TOUCHED BY THE TAJ — MEETING SOME HIJRAS
A horny young man named Somboon

Suzy Size had hired a private driver to bring her from Jaipur to Agra (about US$70) where the undisputed highlight of India — the famous Taj Mahal — was waiting to be discovered.

On the way she made two stops, one at another famous fort — she cannot even remember the name after seeing so many architectural marvels during her five-week trip — where she dutifully had a look at yet another architectural wonder. The other stop was at Keoladeo National Park, which is a World Cultural and Natural Heritage Site and a very worthwhile visit as well.

Suzy Size arrived in Agra — which is nothing special; just one more ugly, polluted Indian city with open sewage — and went to see the Taj Mahal the next day. And it was no surprise: visiting the marvellous Taj was certainly the climactic experience on this culturally so rich (but sexually so poor) journey.

Should Suzy write an ode on the Taj Mahal as many other touched visitors have done? It is not really her field of expertise and she sincerely thinks too much bad poetry has been produced already, including her invention of Neo Dadaism, in praise of her one and only Troy. Her intention is to highlight the gay Indian things which are much more difficult to detect than cultural highlights.

After arriving in Agra, Suzy checked her emails at the complimentary internet computer in the lobby of her hotel. In the corner of her eyes she suddenly saw something moving. It was a mouse!

Suzy jumped up in the air, screamed a bit and pointed to the mouse, but the hotel staff only laughed. Suzy, feeling a bit like a fool, went on a walk around town in order to get a first impression of the Taj Mahal from afar, which is closed to visitors in the evening.

She knew her hotel was close to the Taj, but got the direction wrong. Finally, she gave in to one of the many offers from bicycle rickshaw drivers and let one of them drive your heroine around.

As you might have suspected, gay India tourist, this driver was young (20 years of age) and cute. He soon asked the question one is always asked in India: "Are you married?"

A "no" is always greeted with disbelief in India, but this lad named Somboon did not have that reaction. It took little time for Suzy to find out that he loved to fuck girls, but had also once fucked a male Japanese tourist at the request of the latter. Somboon was versatile, in a way.

Suzy fell firstly for his pretty face. And secondly, for his juicy ass.

Somboon offered to drive your heroine to different shops after having shown her the Taj Mahal from afar this early evening.

He was very frank with Suzy: it did not matter whether or not she was buying anything, but for the delivery of a possible customer, he would get 10 Rupees (US 20 cents) and a 2% commission of any sale, if one should occur.

Suzy played along, and went to a marble shop where they worked on that slightly transparent white Taj Mahal marble, reproducing motifs from that great edifice. She let them explain in detail their working methods, and drank the sweet Indian tea with milk they offered. She looked at the lamps they produced, even though she thought the items to be too much on the kitschy side. Another 10 Rupees for Somboon. Another look on that godly ass of his for Miss Size, while Somboon was pedalling.

Suzy was taken to a jewellery shop where they even offered her a Kingfisher beer which she could not refuse, but still did not buy any ring with the Star of India or similar stuff. Another 10 Rupees for Somboon. Another look on that godly ass of his for Miss Size, while Somboon was pedalling.

A visit to a carpet shop followed and there they had really beautiful hand-knotted carpets that did not cost much. Suzy hired Somboon (and his godly ass) for the whole of the next day and went back in the evening in his presence (otherwise he would not get said commission) to buy a beautiful carpet, which is now gracing the living room back in Castelgandolfo.

Somboon was punctual the next morning even though he confessed to heavy drinking the night before. He drove your heroine to the gate of the world famous monument of Agra.

There was a group of Thai tourists admiring the beautiful monument and Suzy listened in. They naturally exclaimed: "Suai, suai!" (beautiful, beautiful), posing in that silly, but very lovely Thai way for each others' cameras. Just from watching the group of Thais and listening to their maybe banal, but always cheerful conversations; without them knowing that she understood, your heroine instantly became homesick.

In not too long, this India adventure would end and your heroine was really looking forward to returning to the land of smiles, her beloved Pattaya, where the living is easy.

Somboon took Suzy to Agra Fort, another highlight of this journey through India. Suzy took a close look at this huge monument, wandered around and enjoyed herself.

A large group of Hijras finally caught her attention. Suzy tried not to stare too obviously at them, but is not sure to have succeeded. In Thailand they would be called ladyboys or *gothois*, but in India some are even eunuchs. Nowadays only a few of them have their genitals mutilated, but some still do in a bloody ritual with no anaesthetics used.

They often form families or large groups, where the older, respected 'mother' is the guru and teaches the younger disciples the trade, which is often prostitution, but there is a whole ideology attached to it, which differs from region to region.

Some approach young men in public places, ask them for money and will embarrass or even sexually assault them if nothing is paid. In some parts of India, Hijras are employed by the government to collect taxes. In general, their social prestige is not very high, but that is slowly changing. Looking at the group, Suzy was once again glad not to have been born in India.

Somboon was still driving your heroine around and again she could not help but notice his godly ass while he was pedalling. He was always talking about fucking girls, would have loved to take Suzy to a whorehouse for a threesome (1,000 Rupees or US$20).

Instead, Suzy opted for a beer garden and bought him some beers. He now wanted to get Ganja (marijuana) for your heroine, which was growing uninhibitedly in said beer garden. Suzy had another appetite.

She asked Somboon if he could give her a massage. He said he could not, maybe not really understanding the disguised meaning of the question. Then he wanted to take your heroine to a movie theatre where they were showing straight porn.

Suzy is sure he would have allowed your heroine to give him a blowjob in the darkness of said sad cinema, but it all seemed to be too much on the seedy side for your old heroine.

Suzy Size weighed her options — once more while in India! — and chose something which is normally not her cup of coffee: chastity.

CULTURE SHOCK IN DELHI
Suzy stops searching for gay Delhi — she has had enough

In Delhi, the last straw fell, breaking the camel's back.

Walking around splendid colonial Connaught Place, Suzy Size saw a woman in agony. She might have been between 25 or 30 years of age.

She was sitting on the ground in one of the main squares of Delhi. She was incredibly dirty and both her legs were heavily swollen. She was obviously in deep pain and crying in final desperation.

Some good-hearted Indians gave her a 10 Rupee bill (US 20 cents). She no longer took notice, but continued to cry in that heartbreaking manner. 10 Rupees were no longer making any difference. She was dying very publicly in the centre of Delhi. And nobody did anything. Your heroine did nothing as well.

She was shocked. So long she had been able to ignore all the beggars, all the misery one sees while travelling through India, but she could not block out the horrible scene of that dying woman in Connaught Place any longer. She walked one more round around Connaught Place (which takes about 20 to 30 minutes), deeply disturbed. And at the same corner, the same woman was still crying in that absolutely desperate way.

Suzy Size took a taxi back to her hotel. She had had enough. Your heroine hardly left her Delhi hotel again until she could catch her flight the next afternoon. It was culture shock. It came late, but it was intense.

When Suzy Size travelled from Agra to New Delhi, she took a bus. Your circumspect heroine wanted to buy the ticket (or make a reservation) a day before her departure, but was told this was not necessary.

When she arrived at the shabby bus station in the morning, they could not sell her a ticket at the counter, but told her she should purchase it from the conductor on the bus.

When the run-down (but air-conditioned) bus finally departed, there were initially only 7 passengers onboard and the price for the ticket was 180 Rupees (US$3.60). The windows were incredibly dirty; one could hardly see through them. The whole bus operation was visibly overstaffed, highly inefficient and apparently a pet project of the Congress party to employ some supporters. The whole journey of about 200 kilometres took more than five hours.

Some *tuk tuk* drivers at the bus station in New Delhi almost started a fistfight over who was to drive your heroine to her hotel. Welcome to Delhi!

The hotel was located quite centrally, near the well-known Fortis Jessa Ram hospital, within walking distance from Karol Bagh Metro station. Suzy first explored the neighbourhood a bit and soon discovered a nice pub, which became her headquarters during her stay in Delhi.

The streets around Karol Bagh are busy and shops of all kinds are located here. This is a shopping area with a McDonald's and Pizza Hut, but not posh in the Western sense. Beggars, potholes and dirt are everywhere.

Walking further towards Connaught Place, Suzy got lost and was suddenly in a slum. Countless people were camping along the street, the mandatory open sewage system filling the air with foul odours. Several women beggars molested your heroine. Suzy had enough and jumped into a *tuk tuk*, fleeing the scene.

When approaching Connaught Place, the *tuk tuk* stopped near a red light. A little girl dressed like a clown performed handstands and other dangerous gymnastic exercises in the narrow space between the *tuk tuk* and a bus, begging for bread. Suzy as usual tried to ignore that poor girl, but the ignoring act became more and more difficult the longer she was in India.

At first glance, Suzy liked Connaught Place. But while walking around, your heroine was approached all the time. When arriving at a new corner, somebody would explain the obvious: "This is Block G, Sir. What are you looking for?"

Suzy was looking for nothing in particular.

"Do you want to visit Emporium Shopping Centre, Sir? It is very close and I can bring you there free of charge."

Suzy had no such plans. And she did not want to buy one item and get five instead, as advertised on a sign.

Suzy had had enough of all that noise, the filth, the cows, the begging children and parents, the constant hassle. And she no longer had any intention to visit any so-called gay bars that would turn out to not be gay bars in the Western sense, but sorry places where — with some luck — an acquaintance could be made, maybe.

Suzy did not visit 'Pegs and Pints' in Delhi, which is supposed to be the most active gay bar in India — maybe the only one worth a visit.

This dying woman! It was just one ugly scene too much.

Suzy fled the scene. She finished *Half a Life* by V. S. Naipaul in the privacy of her quiet and air-conditioned hotel room that night. She had some strong Kingfisher beers, too.

The hotel clerk that bought the beer for her offered himself for fun, but Suzy Size just wanted to be alone.

"GIVE MY LOVE TO BANGKOK"
A unique hotel in Kolkata

When Suzy Size arrived in Kolkata late in the evening, she boarded another one of those prepaid taxis at the airport to bring her to the Fairlawn Hotel in Sudder Street.

There was no question whether or not your heroine wanted an air-conditioned taxi, since they seem to only have the other sort in Kolkata. Suzy sat in one of those old-fashioned Ambassador Classic cars, with the windows wide open to have some hot air blown into her face, which was better than no air at all.

It was humid, hot and very dark outside. The suburbs of Kolkata are not very well lit, and neither is the rest of this gigantic city. No beggars molested your heroine through the open windows at red lights; it was probably just too late for that.

Suzy had feared her late arrival in Kolkata; she prefers to arrive in broad daylight in cities that are completely unknown to her. And Kolkata has a bad reputation when it comes to poverty and gigantic slums.

Through the internet she had booked a single room at the Fairlawn and they had promised to hold it for her. But would they really do so?

After some minor problems, the taxi driver finally found the Fairlawn, which was established in 1936. Suzy loved it at first glance. She entered through the one and only garden entrance — an older, almost frail helper had taken her bags — and felt thrown back in time when the English colonialists still had the say in India. Today, the Fairlawn still looks like it did when it opened shortly before the outbreak of World

War II. There was comfortable old-fashioned rattan furniture in the lobby, and many photographs on the walls showed famous (and forgotten) people who stayed at this charming hotel. Some guests were having drinks in the garden restaurant.

At the reception, they found your heroine's reservation with no problems. They had written all the details of her email booking by hand in one of those huge reservation books, which have become most rare in the modern hotel industry of today. They had given away all the other single rooms to other customers, but allocated Suzy Size with a large and comfortable room with three beds right beside the dining room instead.

In other, more sexually-developed countries, it would have been no problem at all to find some attractive companions to fill the other two beds, but here in Kolkata Suzy doubted she could accomplish this arduous task.

The bathtub was huge and, as advertised, they had added a huge boiler many years back to provide their distinguished guests with hot water that could flow through an old tropical shower head. Air conditioning and TVs had been added at a later stage and the same applies to a family-sized refrigerator. But otherwise, time was frozen here.

Suzy was not yet ready for bed and went out for a beer. Sudder Street is very much like those other backpacker tourist streets you find in Jakarta, Kathmandu or Bangkok, but much smaller, since tourism does not seem to be the big currency collector in Kolkata.

Suzy had a couple of beers, listened to the conversations around and finally called it a day. Since your heroine's room was just beside the dining room, Suzy had feared to be woken up in the morning by the noises of other guests who rose earlier than her. But that fear proved to be unnecessary, Suzy could not hear a thing and slept relatively late into the morning.

When finally up, Suzy ordered some eggs and cornflakes plus tea with milk. Not long after, the tea was served by an old waiter in a large pot, which was covered with one of those old-fashioned fluffy fabric things to cover it and keep it warm. Cornflakes are not served every day at the Fairlawn, but this happened to be a cornflakes day (the next one proved to be a porridge day).

The sensation was the fried egg, which was accompanied not only by tomatoes and fried potatoes but, believe it or not, real bacon! Suzy had not been served any pork all over India, even though she had seen many pigs roaming. Your heroine had to eat so much tandoori chicken, butter naan, palak paneer and tasteless lentils of all kinds during her five-week voyage through the subcontinent. She has vowed NEVER AGAIN to eat any of that boring Indian food for the rest of her life. But now all of a sudden, bacon!

After breakfast, Suzy turned in her key at the lobby and was about to leave that great hotel to discover the wonders of Kolkata when she noticed the Fairlawn motto on a sign: "Receive tourists as guests and send them away as friends." This is a quote by Indira Gandhi.

Another sign explained that Bed and Breakfast (Suzy had not booked full board) included the traditional afternoon tea — splendid, indeed.

But then Suzy finally discovered the star of the Fairlawn, who is — without doubt — Violet Smith, who was born in 1921 and who happens to own this unique place. She can be found in the lobby every single day of the year and converses here with her guests, many of whom are or were famous.

Tom Stoppard stayed at the Fairlawn and so did Julie Christie, Penelope Cruz, singer Sting, Guenter Grass and Patrick Swayze, who formed a lasting friendship with Violet Smith when filming *City of Joy* at the hotel.

Suzy Size instantly discovered a soulmate in Violet Smith, who is a restored redhead, always perfectly coiffed and manicured, with thick red lipstick and certainly not hiding her jewellery.

Violet has a sharp mind and a sharp mouth. Due to a clever long-term contract, the old hotelier only has to pay 700 Rupees (US$14) a month in rent for her unique premises. Charming Violet thanked Suzy for taking her picture and explained why she only had one child — a daughter — with the late Major Ted Smith, whom she married in Kolkata in 1944: "My husband was a cricket player, you know?"

Does Suzy really know? What did Violet Smith mean with those odd or cryptic words? Are cricket players more interested in the company of their fellow cricket players than their wives?

Might that be the reason the couple only had one child during their marriage, which lasted decades? We might never know; Suzy did not really dare to ask.

Your heroine did her homework in Kolkata. She went on the usual sightseeing in a rickshaw pulled by a barefoot man. She — after having recovered from her Delhi/India culture shock — even dutifully checked out the so-called gay bars of Kolkata.

She had a beer at Sams and at Olypub, but skipped the discos and all the other outlets at the Park Hotel. All these are listed as gay places in the relevant guides. All were walking distance to the Fairlawn Hotel.

It would probably be easy to bring a local talent to the hotel. All this makes the Fairlawn the natural place to stay in Kolkata. And you can meet Violet Smith who, upon the departure of your heroine, begged Suzy Size: "Give my love to Bangkok."

And Suzy did just that, with pleasure.

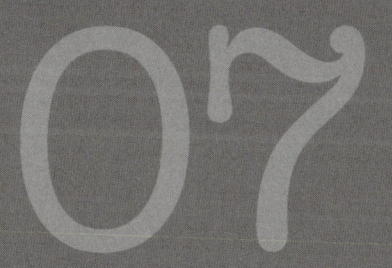

BOAT RACES
Thailand

07

THE FAMOUS BOAT RACES OF NONG KHAI
A mighty pretext for fun, fun, fun

With the end of Buddhist Lent, by the beginning of October, the annual boat races take place all over Thailand.

Suzy Size has seen many of them over the years in Nong Khai, where she has a second majestic residence called Castelgandolfo II, built on land bought from the family of her beloved boyfriend of so many years, Khun Amorn.

At first, Khun Amorn had not wanted to come along, due to some extremely important parties in Pattaya, but was now cheerful since there were also extremely important parties scheduled up in Nong Khai.

He drove far too fast as always; Suzy suffered many near-death experiences during the journey up to Nong Khai, and screamed hysterically quite a bit, but somehow survived.

Only once were they stopped by a policeman, who rightly accused Khun Amorn of speeding, without having a machine to prove this offence. But who needs such a useless machine in a country where everyone is speeding anyhow?

Is it not the friendlier solution — beneficial to both parties involved — to agree on a small penalty of 100 Baht (US$3.20)? *Chivit paeng*, life is expensive, right?

The 100 Baht bill is handed over discreetly and — it goes without saying — no red tape (like painstakingly writing a receipt) is involved.

And to make up for the little delay, Khun Amorn will naturally do more speeding.

If you have never been to Nong Khai, gay tourist to Asia, do not expect too many wonders. You may visit the Buddhist Monster Park, of course, the Tasadej, the Indochina Market, and the beautiful shores of the mighty Mekong, but there is no structured gay scene.

You will meet many beautiful sons of Nong Khai in Pattaya or Bangkok, but close to home, most of them become shy again, and would not like to be reminded how they earn their money in Jomtien beach or in some of the gay Bangkok massage places. They can become gay if you pay, but this wonder works best far from home.

Khun Amorn is not such a guy after living with your heroine for many, many years. He is openly gay, shamelessly obvious when he wants to make a catch. Like with that cute waiter with the ponytail whom he showered with funny compliments, in one of the many hot pot restaurants that open at night along the shores of the Mekong. (It is far too hot during the day, so they open only at night.)

It is owned by a friend of Khun Amorn and both were teasing that young man with the pony tail, although both knew that he has "a wife already". They had him in the past, maybe, but now it was a harmless game only, since he has "a wife already".

Later that night, Khun Amorn and his friend (who likes to dress as a woman) went for a drinking and hunting spree to the Lao Thai Hotel with a disco. Khun Amorn came home in the early morning and had to sleep all day in order to recover.

But do not worry too much about Khun Amorn, he was certainly fit enough the next day to do some hearty gambling with his friends on the beautiful terrace overlooking the fishpond. He had talked your heroine into going to town in order to buy noodle soup at a very special noodle shop. It is no boast: you will truly get the world's best noodle soup at said shop in Nong Khai!

Normally, Khun Amorn will cook something for his friendly old parents at noon, but he had some other priorities this day. By seducing Suzy Size to go for the noodle soup, he killed several birds with one stone. Your heroine was out of the way when the gambling started (she hates it and has complained loudly about it in the past) and could get the food for his parents without further endeavours on his part or him having to pay for it.

Upon her return to the house, Suzy would be so happy about her great noodle soup, she would not moan too much about that despicable gambling, and instead have a Beer Chang with ice. She could even be approached for a little soft loan of 40 Baht — for good luck, mainly. And it helped Khun Amorn indeed. He won about 150 Baht that incredibly lucky day.

When some friends had to go to the airport in Udon Thani, Suzy Size and Khun Amorn gave them a ride. Suzy had seen a sign for a new Carrefour store when driving by Udon Thani and lusted after some of the excellent pork sausages she frequently buys in their Pattaya outlet.

After the drop-off at the airport, Khun Amorn was ordered to search for Carrefour. Since he is incredibly lazy, he tried to convince Suzy to try the Tesco Lotus outlet nearby. But your heroine insisted on Carrefour, not least for their delicious bread as well.

Suzy told Khun Amorn to ask someone for the way to Carrefour, but as usual, the stubborn (not so young anymore) man would not do that. Firstly, he could lose face by not knowing where Carrefour in Udon Thani might be. Secondly, the person asked might not know the answer and could thus also lose face.

Khun Amorn drove for about 45 minutes through the heavy Friday evening traffic of Udon Thani without any clue, no sign of Carrefour in sight. Eventually, he bought a flower garland from one of the sellers and asked for directions. When they finally reached Carrefour after well over an hour, it was merely a two-minute drive away from the airport. To add insult to injury, Carrefour in Udon Thani had neither those delicious sausages, nor that crunchy bread!

The highlight of this visit to Nong Khai was, without doubt, the famous boat races. The extended family and many friends first gathered at the house of Khun Amorn's niece, just a stone's throw from the Mekong. Beer and whisky were drunk at the occasion and many snacks tasted. While Suzy stuck to potato chips and peanuts, the locals tried fried silk worms and other ethnic specialties. Everyone was chatting and Khun Amorn and his two gay friends had a good time joking with the others.

Then it was time to proceed to the banks of the Mekong just walking distance away. It was awfully hot and Suzy — as the honorary main sponsor of Khun Amorn's family and group — soon sat down at a table in the shade and ordered food and drinks of all sorts.

Once in while a boat race would take place and people actually got up and cheered a bit, but the boat races are not the main point, they are merely a pretext to have a good time. Drinking, eating, talking and joking is equally fun as seeing and being seen. And betting, of course, is great fun too.

The same drunk as last year tried to chat (in strange English) with your heroine and asked the same banal questions as last year. If Suzy is there next year, there is a high chance he will be there again and ask the same questions anew.

One major change, however, is that there were many more young *gothois* (ladyboys) out there this year. One of them is a 15-year-old nephew of Khun Amorn, who has been effeminate since he was five years of age. Another young nephew is not sure yet if he will join the Gothoi Association of Nong Khai, but the seasoned eyes of Suzy Size say: most probably.

A cute, young *gothoi* who had already caught an old and really ugly Farang flirted restlessly with your heroine behind the back of said man. Suzy was flattered, but was more interested in the manly rowers who were busy with the famous boat races and not into hanky panky right now.

Suzy will surely see some of them back on Jomtien beach.

BIG FISH IN CHINA
China, Laos

08

WHY NOT?
Lost in Shenzhen

Leaving her new little girl friend for China was not as easy as first expected. Suzy Size actually shed a tear or two when taking a last look at Champa, the lovely kitten Khun Amorn had saved from a garbage bin and since taken excellent care of. Young cats are so funny and cute.

But, alas, duty called. As you know, gay fellow tourist, the mission of your restless heroine on her infamous Gay Friendship Tour is to describe Asia, and maybe later the whole world, from that specific gay perspective. And Suzy has not been to (Mainland) China — a giant in every respect — for at least 15 years. Back then, she had travelled from Saigon all the way to Beijing by train.

But a new perspective on China — this huge blind spot on the world gay map, with literally millions of cute and horny men — needed your dedicated sentinel's urgent attention. This time she was starting in Shenzhen and then travelling up the coast, again by railway (if not too tired), to Beijing.

And later? Time (and Suzy) will tell.

Shenzhen, the industrial city just across the border from Hong Kong, is a boom town with about 10 million inhabitants. Suzy Size had booked an inexpensive ticket on Air Asia for herself and her older sister, Magna Size, who was coming along.

Magna's boyfriend picked up Suzy at Castelgandolfo and drove the two ladies to the Bangkok airport. Through the internet they had made a reservation for the first two nights at some hotel at US$23 per night.

The half-empty plane took off as scheduled at 6.50pm and arrived punctually at 10.50pm local time (an hour ahead of Thailand) at Shenzhen airport. The passengers were asked to stay seated and some Chinese medical personnel with mouth masks entered the plane and measured the body temperature of all passengers. Suzy and Magna passed this challenging test and were finally allowed into China amidst the obvious hysteria about the swine flu.

The immigration and baggage procedures went smoothly and in no time the two chatty ladies were in a taxi — the second taxi driver had agreed to turn on the meter.

The ride took almost an hour and cost 200 Yuan (US$1 was worth about 7 Yuan) including the highway fees. There were some hawkers near the hotel and the two ladies went for some drinks there. There were open air pool tables too and the young men bending deeply over them attracted the attention of your two heroines.

Magna — if this is possible — was staring even harder at those juicy Chinese asses than Suzy. The bill for three big bottles of beer and two cokes was absolutely incredible: 20 Yuan (not even US$3!).

The first thing the next morning, the two sisters went for an exploratory walk in search of the centre of Shenzhen. They were building a Metro line in the neighbourhood where a lot of construction (and destruction) was going on. The two girls finally found a decent coffee shop near a McDonald's and thought this might be the town centre. But where was the darn Jing Du Hotel?

Suzy had read somewhere that a gay Shenzhen bar 'Why Not?' was behind the Jing Du Hotel and the minimum target set by your two heroines was to find this bar with the interesting name during their time in Shenzhen.

While walking the streets, they were smiled at by some mature but still good-looking gay Chinese guys. The two ladies waved back at them, but were not followed. After spending almost three hours walking, they opted for a nap first and to continue their important gay search later.

Diligent Suzy had done her homework back in Castelgandolfo. She had consulted the Gay Guide of her choice and visited the website of cute masseur Daniel Yao — only to find out he had moved from Shenzhen to Singapore. Could he not have waited a while before taking such a drastic step?

She had also visited the website of Chinastar Massage and was aroused by the prospect of calling over one of those incredible hunks. But then she also read the comments left by online users: apparently this service sends over guys — who are much less stunning — other than those depicted on the site.

Then Suzy had contacted another of the many therapist websites, one named Chinahandsomeboy, which had 34 very interesting massage boys within Shenzhen alone. Suzy had asked for prices and they had actually responded: they wanted 800 Yuan (about US$115) plus the taxi fare for their massage service — a bit steep, Suzy thought.

But contrary to predominantly vegetarian India, meat would at least be available in China, if the urge became unbearable. Suzy could have easily found gay Smart Jack Bar in Shenzhen which had its own website with a readable map, but no, Why Not was in her stubborn head and had to be found at all possible cost!

Magna supported her younger sister greatly in this arduous task, but first they wanted to visit the train station to enquire about trains to Guangzhou (formerly Canton), where they were headed to the next day, and boarded a taxi. It was only then that the two sisters realised that their hotel was located in a suburb of gigantic Shenzhen. It would have taken them a hundred years to walk to the centre of town!

At the hotel reception they had gotten a map and had somebody circle the exact location of Jing Du Hotel, which was more or less within walking distance from the train station. After enquiring about the train tickets, they walked towards the hotel.

But, after getting lost many times, unable to read a single word of Chinese and asking several people for directions, the darn hotel that they found was the Oriental Regent. After some confusion, the ladies found out that the Oriental Regent was the (former) Jing Du Hotel!

Was Why Not supposed to be behind Jing Du Hotel? What did 'behind' mean? Was this when facing the entrance of the hotel? Or when looking at it from the other side? Or perhaps they meant beside?

Your heroines, Magna and Suzy Size, walked all around the big Oriental Regent of Shenzhen. The two grey girls looked into many dark and lit alleys alike. They enquired in many nightclubs if they housed elusive Why Not on their third floor, but nobody in the area had ever heard of bloody, bloody Why Not.

It was a conundrum why nobody had heard of Why Not. Your tired heroine Suzy was really out of her wits, but Magna proved to be a very persistent assistant indeed. It was Magna who asked all those watchmen, all those bystanders. None spoke or understood more than a few words of English at best. Had there been any policemen around, Magna would most certainly have asked them too.

Suzy saw two gay men walking by. A smile was exchanged and then Suzy ran after them and asked them about the location of Why Not. The direction they pointed in was the street just behind the entrance of the Regent Oriental. That is where your two sentinels had been looking already, but of course, they went back and tried again. Nobody knew the place, and there was no trace of any sign in English.

Clever Magna enquired in a fancy hair salon nearby, but all those cute hairdressers did not seem to understand what the two Farang ladies were looking for. Instead, they handed a piece of paper to Magna with the question: "What color do you want?"

But finally, one of them seemed to understand and to know where Why Not was. He pointed to the same spot as the two gay guys had before.

In a last heroic attempt they tried again, but still could not find that damned Why Not. Suzy was on the brink of a nervous breakdown and close to giving up, but Magna finally entered a shop and asked the receptionist if she knew where it was. She did not and the tired ladies finally gave up and walked away. But they were followed by a young man who had just walked into the previous shop. He took Magna's arm and led her back. They entered the same shop Magna had just enquired at and took the elevator up to second floor. And there it was at last — Why Not!

The entrance of Why Not was on the second floor, not — as they had printed on their name card — on the third. It is a friendly club spanning two stories, and on top of the bar or disco is the karaoke lounge. Suzy had a glass of beer for 30 Yuan. It was a bit boring though, since Magna and Suzy were the only guests. Not really the reason they had come here. The two very tired ladies left soon.

Would Suzy Size go back to Why Not? Why not, now that she has learned where it is — the hard way. But unfortunately, Why Not went out of business shortly after the Size sisters' visit.

"HUOCHEZHAN ZAI NAR?"
A splendid train ride to Guangzhou

Besides *'ni hao'* (hello) and *'xiexie'* (thanks), your heroine Suzy Size is not too fluent in Mandarin. Years ago, when she travelled from Saigon to Beijing entirely by train, she had acquired a Chinese phrase book and learnt the following very important sentence (the only one she can remember in her present semi-senile state of mind): *"Huochezhan zai nar?"* It means: "Where is the train station?" This is certainly a very vital question if you want to travel up the coast from Shenzhen to Beijing, in a country where people are not very fluent in English.

When the two ladies left their Shenzhen hotel — not early in the morning since both are night birds rather than early risers — they flagged down a taxi and Suzy said: *"Huochezhan!"*

The driver did not get it at first and looked puzzled, if not distressed, at Suzy. Only when she handed him the piece of paper she had acquired at the reception that spelled "*Huochezhan*" in Chinese characters, was he finally able to understand. He repeated: "*Huochezhan!*" with a foolish grin (exactly how Suzy had told that Chinese imbecile initially), and when both Suzy and Magna nodded simultaneously, he drove off toward the Shenzhen train station.

Both Suzy and Magna — who has seen a great part of the world herself — were thrilled when they arrived at ultramodern Shenzhen train station. Not only is everything spick and span, next door is the huge bus terminal. The different means of public transport are well intertwined here, as they should be worldwide. In no time your two greying (but cheerful) heroines got their tickets at 75 Yuan each (less than US$11) from the ticket counter for train D7028 from Shenzhen to Guangzhou (formerly Canton). It was leaving at 12.05pm, and they had seat 029 and seat 030 in coach 3.

Like everyone else your two heroines had to have their bags screened at one of those machines at the airport. All their items in the suitcases, Magna's mega-size dandruff shampoo and Suzy's many condoms and 7 tubes of gliding cream passed without the least problems through this benevolent (and understanding) machine.

After an hour-long train ride — the maximum speed noticed was 201 km/h — the two ladies arrived in the Eastern Train Station of Guangzhou.

At a hotel reservation desk in that brand-new train station they found a hotel at 230 RMB or Yuan (about US$33) a night, including free transport. It was supposed to be close to the old train station where the train for Xiamen — the next Chinese destination — was to leave.

After checking in, your two heroines boarded a taxi and headed towards the Cathedral — yes, they really have such a place in Guangzhou built in the 19th century by the French. Suzy had proposed visiting the Cathedral, not for religious reasons, being agnostic, but Cathedrals are often in the centre of old towns — thus being a good place to start an exploration, and so it was in Guangzhou too.

There was an interesting, vibrant market with dried seafood of all kinds — minus the smell — where they also sold an incredible variety of nuts (walnuts for instance) and big piles of Chinese 'Parma' ham. The old part of Canton — or Guangzhou — is really worth a visit.

Nearby is the famous Pearl River and Magna had the idea to go on a cruise — river cruise that is, gay fellow tourist — and it was sheer pleasure at minimal expense.

There was a strange fellow on that boat, a good-looking young man that smiled at Suzy and Magna when they got on the top of the large boat. He was sitting at a table not too far from your two heroines, had a bag with him and looked like a student. He was walking around on that boat, but always looked at Suzy and Magna, maybe more at Magna than at Suzy (to her chagrin). Finally, he sat down at their table.

He started to play with Magna's hand, obviously fascinated by her body hair, moving up to the arm, touching it again and again. But the fellow seemed to be very tired, his whole upper body was flat on the table, and he closed his eyes as if asleep. Then he seemed to wake up again and talked to himself in Chinese. Suzy and Magna just looked at each other.

Magna finally pointed out, "The elevator does not go to the top floor."

Was it due to some illegal drugs he had taken? Or was he just nuts? We will never know. But what a pity, such a good-looking boy!

What else was there in Guangzhou? Suzy and Magna went to the bar street on the bank of the Pearl River. This is a place where lots of bars, restaurants and inexpensive hotels are located.

If she were to return to Guangzhou, Suzy would probably opt for the Youth Hostel, which offers fine accommodation at inexpensive rates. If you stay there you are in the middle of the nightlife with lots of young and attractive men, so you may feel young again. Your two restless heroines went to Shamian Island as well, a former concession where the Westerners were banned to; no Chinese were allowed there. Apparently it can be cruisy at times, but it was constantly raining when your two heroines were in Guangzhou, so no action could be observed.

The old train station was not the place where the train to Xiamen was leaving from after all, but it was definitely worth a visit. Lots of migrant workers were waiting for trains in huge queues, rough people with reddish peasant faces and their belongings in bundles, not suitcases.

The two ladies went to the Orchid Garden where Suzy discovered *parmentiera alata*, a tree that produces flowers that look like little cocks. Naturally, she liked that tree...

To kill time until the overnight train for Xiamen was leaving that evening, Suzy and Magna walked through the fantastic huge Yuexiu Park, just across the Orchid Garden. If the weather had been fine, they most certainly would have headed for the swimming pool in search of Guangzhou male beauty, but with the overcast sky (constantly on the verge of rain) this was not a tempting idea.

How about the gay life of Guangzhou? Suzy and Magna have to admit, they were neither successful, nor did they really try hard. All existing gay guides consulted were not very useful, the places listed were described so vaguely; it was nearly impossible to find them with the given directions.

Your two heroines left interesting Guangzhou without the gay experience. It was only on the next day when they had reached Xiamen, that Suzy received the following mail from Tom, one of her blog readers: "If you ever decide to come to Guangzhou, give me a call. I would like to meet you and invite you to dinner at my place. I have read about all your adventures."

Suzy is definitely tempted to return to nice Guangzhou one of these days. She only hopes for some sunshine then.

THE SHRINKING AND RISING FEELING
Good old-fashioned cruising around very gay Xiamen pier

After the 14-hour train ride from Guangzhou to Xiamen, Magna and Suzy Size arrived again at a *Huochezhan* or *Zhan* in the morning.

Not knowing that there were soft sleepers, the two old ladies had bought a hard sleeper for 261 Yuan (US$37). There are three berths on each side of the compartment, but Magna and Suzy — to their chagrin — were left alone all night.

Suzy had a very hard night behind her when they finally arrived in Xiamen, which is located on a large island with the same name. Not a hard night, because of the hard sleeper, but because she fell sick, threw up and suffered from the runs in that very basic train bathroom with no proper sit-down toilet. Well, your heroine managed somehow and off in a taxi the two sisters went, to the scenic part of Xiamen which is located opposite the pier.

If you go to Xiamen, just head for Lujiang Harbourview Hotel. This beautiful old hotel is, in a way, to Xiamen what the Negresco is to Nice. It is located right opposite the pier, on the first row of the majestic boulevard facing the sea, an area quite reminiscent of places in the French Riviera.

Your two heroines directed the taxi there and enquired about the room rates inside said hotel. The published room rates in China are almost always far too high; in other words, you can easily bargain them down.

The cheapest room they were offered at the Lujiang cost 310 Yuan (US$44), but it was really small and the window faced the wall of the building just behind; not a great view.

Magna and Suzy (who both travel on a budget) made the extra effort to walk a bit further and just behind the Lujiang they found a decent room for 168 Yuan. There was no wifi at the hotel, but the two resourceful ladies soon found a nice café with free wifi for its guests just around the corner.

The owner, a motherly Chinese woman, spoke English quite well and was obviously proud of her linguistic achievements. Your two travellers tapped on her knowledge immediately and had her write the address of Tong Yin bar and the name of the Lu Jiang movie theatre in Chinese on a piece of paper.

She looked at your two heroines in a funny way and asked them why they wanted to go there of all places. Where, she wondered, did the two strangers get these names or addresses from?

Oh, from the internet, your two heroines replied. Both tried to look as innocent as two newborn babies. They did not reveal to that friendly and motherly Chinese woman that Tong Yin was a gay bar and on the third floor of the Lu Jiang movie theatre was Yin He (Silver River), a gay sauna.

The woman was obviously puzzled. She probably had been instructed by the Chinese authorities — like all her countrymen and women — to only show the 'nice side' of China to foreigners.

When your two heroines returned to the café the next day, she asked whether they had found those places and, again, where they had gotten those names from? Magna and Suzy did not want to disappoint her and answered: Yes, they found those places. But they were very strange indeed! And, under no circumstances, would they ever go back there. Which is true, in a way.

Tong Ying bar had closed down and the premises were deserted. And your two gay sentinels had easily found Lu Jiang, which was a porn movie theatre nearby. That explained why that friendly woman had wondered about the good reputation (or even sanity) of those two Farangs.

They had found said theatre easily after showing people on the streets the piece of paper with its name. But it must be said, they garnered many strange looks. And right there, on third floor, was a door that surely must lead to gay heaven: Silver River gay sauna was waiting for a cruise.

The entrance fee of 30 Yuan was moderate indeed, and your two heroines got undressed in no time, took a shower and started to take a closer look at the local talent. But alas, there were only old and even older men!

They were very friendly grandpas and were all interested in those two sexy strangers with all that exotic body hair. They touched your heroines on the arms, tried to squeeze or even suck a tit, fingering through the breast hair and going for the cocks with their grabbing hands.

Suzy immediately experienced that shrinking feeling. Her cock shrunk to a never-seen-before size, as if he wanted to return to the safety of the surrounding body. Her cock was hastily fleeing the grabbing hands of all those friendly, but very old men.

Suzy escaped them and went on the internet, looked at some revealing pictures of Brazilian hustlers. Some of the Chinese grandpas looked over her shoulder and were quite amazed.

Magna had a worse destiny: she fell asleep on a bed in the darker area and was seriously molested by the Chinese hordes, who took advantage of her moment of weakness...

Suzy went back the next day and entered the sex theatre downstairs. Even straight porn cinemas are sometimes rewarding for the gay traveller.

That day, they were showing a ghost movie for three customers. They have double seats in the theatre and as soon as Suzy sat down, a female whore sat beside her and offered a massage. Of course, she was refuted. When a second woman offered more of the same, Suzy left.

What else was there to do in Xiamen? Eat some of that delicious fresh seafood available all over. Stroll through the many interesting roads. Take the ferry over to Gu Lang Yu, an island visible from Xiamen Pier, and stroll around that beautiful place. The ride is free for bottoms — if you stay downstairs, that is — and costs 1 Yuan for the upper deck. The ride back from the island to Xiamen is 8 Yuan (bottom) and an additional 1 Yuan for the upper deck. Magna and Suzy, both being notorious tops, shouldered the enormous expenses for the upper deck.

And then, of course, you can embark on some good old-fashioned cruising. The whole area around the pier (and the pier toilet) is very cruisy at night.

Suzy saw one guy she liked in the toilet and followed his juicy ass around. At one point she stood right beside him, but he proved to merely be a cock teaser and left. Suzy gave up on him and when he came back later, your heroine was no longer interested in that obvious bitch. Another one with thick fingers — not long, not short, a bit like a gorilla — sat down next to your heroine. He had such fleshy fingers. Suzy could see his cock through those fingers and would have loved to take a bite.

They held hands there on that bench with lots of people around, but it was rather dark. Nobody looked at them or took notice, or worse, offence. He could not speak a single word of English, and mentioned something about a karaoke, but Suzy decided against hanky panky. This, younger gay tourist, is the advantage of old age: things must no longer happen at any price or any inconvenience.

But then yet another acquaintance was made, an absolutely good-looking young man stood beside Suzy at the fence, glaring out at the sea. Suddenly, their fingers touched.

Both played around a while and now the fact that this angel could not speak any English either bore no importance for your heroine. She just felt that rising feeling beside that wonderful young man, quite contrary to her shrinking feeling in that silly sauna.

Her hotel was just around the corner and Suzy wanted to show this example of immaculate Xiamen manhood her prized stamp collection. He actually followed your lucky heroine into the hotel. The reception girl looked a bit puzzled, but did not object when the two happy people entered the elevator.

Suzy entered and locked the door of the room. But when she tried to kiss him, he suddenly signalled NO, with his hands. He wanted to leave at once. Suzy walked him out. The reception girl looked relieved.

Sad Suzy went back to the pier area and, for a moment, pondered jumping into the moody waters, to end that miserable life of hers right there. But then — thank God — she decided, the show must go on. She wanted to see more of China.

Instead of killing herself, she had a beer at one of the seafood restaurants nearby. Incredibly, it only cost 5 Yuan. Naturally, your heroine had a second and even a third.

TREASURE HUNTS IN HANGZHOU
Lose your hearts in Hangzhou

Having lived in Thailand for almost 20 years, Suzy Size tends to forget the importance of weather in other less sun-blessed countries. If the rains fall in Pattaya, you just wait until it stops before you go out.

But when your two brave heroines arrived in Hangzhou — after a marvellous and scenic 22-hour train ride — from Xiamen, this time in a much more comfortable 'soft sleeper', it started to pour. And the rain was cold, which was a terrible difference from warm Thailand.

The first thing they did at Hangzhou Huochezhan at around 9am was to have breakfast at KFC — which is certainly less glamourous than breakfast at Tiffany's — but just fine. The coffee is always of drinkable quality, and in China they offer those delicious small egg tarts originally introduced to the country by the Portuguese in Macau. And the prices are not outrageous like at Starbucks; a coffee and a tart are available for just 11 Yuan (US$1.60).

After the refreshments, they braved the cold and crippling rain and tried to get a taxi outside the train station. Since none of the relevant Gay Guides for China offered any recommendations for accommodation, they had consulted their *Lonely Planet* and thought Dongpo Hotel to be a reasonable choice because of its location near Westlake, which is the main attraction of Hangzhou.

But because of that nasty cold rain, the taxi drivers tried to take advantage of your two gay sentinels. They wanted 50 Yuan instead of the usual 10 Yuan to drive them there. Soaking wet, they finally agreed to pay 40 Yuan and off they went.

Had they stayed within the train station, they could have easily caught a regular metered taxi from the queue. Not once during this whole China trip were your two heroines ever overcharged by taxi drivers otherwise. On the contrary, the drivers all tried very hard to find the requested location, which at times was difficult due to the lack of communication.

When they reached Dongpo Hotel, it was closed for a major renovation. Suzy parked Magna in the lobby of a nearby expensive hotel and went, armed with her quite useless umbrella, in search of inexpensive accommodation for the two sisters.

Elan Inn was a good choice. The branch they selected near Westlake is part of a chain, which offers simple but practical accommodation at a reasonable price (186 Yuan for a double, about US$26, including a bottle of water on weekdays, but strangely enough, not on weekends or holidays).

The rooms of your two heroines were located opposite each other; they had no real windows to the outside world, but windows facing the corridor instead. So when Suzy sat at her laptop later — connected to the world through a cable — she could see Magna do the same on the other side, if both of them opted to open their curtains.

That rainy day, Suzy decided to stay in most of the time, just leaving briefly to have something to eat and drink, but otherwise doing her usual daily routine on the internet. But that was not as simple as it seemed, since several gay websites were banned in Hangzhou. Thank god Suzy had printed out all relevant information regarding gay places in China back in Castelgandolfo!

The next day, when the general mood was much better since the sun was shining, your two restless heroines went for a gay treasure hunt through lovely Hangzhou.

This huge Westlake really is a marvel. It is pure pleasure to walk around its well-kept shores with all those trees and plants cared for by diligent masses of gardeners. Older people play cards in some areas. In others there are hobby musicians playing for hobby singers.

One could rent a bike and thus circle the lake or cross over by boat. Suzy and Magna had initially assumed to stay for two nights or so in beautiful Hangzhou, but finally opted for four: they both obviously lost their heart to Hangzhou and would return anytime, provided the sun is shining.

There is, by the way, some cruising going on in front of the Overseas Chinese Hotel, which is located right on the lakefront. Suzy and Magna must have spent hours there just enjoying that wonderful place, looking at some juicy asses and trying to make that infamous eye contact.

Magna — probably even more desperate to get laid than Suzy — had done some very important preparatory work during the nasty rain earlier and had finally found the crucial intersection of Baochu and Beishan Road just at the Westlake, but had not been able to locate Han Lin Cun sauna, her actual target.

The descriptions on the traditional Gay Guides for Asia are often cryptic or outright wrong and, following their instructions, you sometimes feel like a treasure hunter trying to read a map full of riddles and conundrums.

On that sunny morning, after the customary breakfast at KFC, your two heroines headed for that most interesting intersection when it comes to gay life in Hangzhou.

This corner is not so difficult to find: if you are lazy, just let a Chinese person you trust write the names of those two streets on a piece of paper and take an inexpensive taxi. Or you can walk towards Westlake and turn right once you reach Overseas Chinese Hotel. From there, it is about a 1 km walk until you reach the intersection of Baochu and Beishan Road.

You then walk along Baochu Road (away from the lake on the right-hand side of the road), until you reach an entertainment complex after about 50 metres — you will have passed Lakeside Hotel on the left side of the road. Suzy and Magna followed the description to the word, but could not find the entrance to the heavenly Han Lin Cun sauna at first. They walked by several times, but the signs — in Chinese only — were not very helpful to your illiterate sisters. But thanks to their great gaydar, they finally found it.

Since it was too early to enter then, your heroines looked for Junchu Club, another gay venue that was supposed to be nearby, but once again could not find it. After visiting the sauna later that evening, they asked another gay Chinese visitor for the way and found it easily then.

From the sauna, head back on Baochu Road towards the lake for just a few metres and turn left into a small alley. You will see a straight bar called Cherry and will have to avoid the female hustlers offering massages like the plague. The next entrance in the building will lead you down to the pleasant Junchu Club, a disco or karaoke bar where the younger gay crowds of Hangzhou gather.

It must be said, those young men were not very interested in your two grey heroines, but were at least friendly and respectful. It is a good place to watch happy younger gay men having fun and to have a drink or two. And you never know, one might want a (sugar) daddy?

Magna is over 60 years old but still has an enormous appetite for sex. While Suzy enjoyed just sitting on the lakeshore, Magna hastily boarded a taxi and had the driver bring her to the corner of Mugangshan Lu and Wen Yi Lu, somewhere in the asphalt jungle of huge Hangzhou.

From there she walked on the right-hand side of Mugangshan Lu, away from the city, for about 600 metres. There, she found the entrance to a park that is full of elder folks during the day, but there are always some gay guys cruising too. Just play the game and see what happens. Magna, who went to the toilet next to the entrance of the park, met a guy right there. He followed her to the park and gave her a blowjob in some bushes.

Naturally, Suzy had to try that as well the next day and would have had her chance to play too, but let it go by due to the lack of beauty. This interesting park — the name is not known to your heroine — is supposed to become really wild after the sun is down. A visit there is certainly more thrilling than knitting.

The entrance fee for Han Lin Cun sauna is 30 Yuan (a bit more than US$4). The sauna is not very large, but it is clean and has all amenities you would expect of such an institution.

Magna got caught by a well-endowed local talent right in the shower room, whereas Suzy — the old, picky queen — was hesitant to accept any of the offers made to her. She finally sat down beside a possible prey, a cute and young Chinese man. He was obviously very shy and just occasionally looked back at your sex-hungry heroine, but quickly returned to his important work on his mobile phone, sending text messages.

He wore short trousers and a T-shirt, and was not half naked like your heroine. Suzy suddenly noticed that he wore a tag around his neck. Inspecting that strange tag, Suzy saw that it had a number 003 on it. He was a masseur, but certainly not one of those pushy guys. (The other professionals at Han Lin Cu are not pushy either.)

With her hands and a lot of other sign language, Suzy found out that one hour of massage cost 200 Yuan (about US$28). You will not be surprised, gay tourist to China, that your newly chaste heroine, who had so far not had too much luck in that great land — remember the humiliation in Xiamen! — immediately agreed to that most interesting and promising deal. Suzy was clearly inspired by Magna, who often says: "Fair exchange is not robbery."

After signing a receipt for 200 Yuan — you pay when leaving the sauna premises — Suzy laid down and that friendly young 22-year-old started to massage the back of a relaxed and happy Suzy Size.

It was not long before his face appeared beside your heroine's and he started kissing like a master of the universe. Needless to say, the traditional part of the massage ended right at that moment.

More cannot be revealed here about this encounter; the censors of Hangzhou are diligent fellows, as you know. They have banned access to several gay websites in their clean town already and might try to block them even countrywide, if dirty lies about superb Hangzhou were told.

HAPPY HOURS AT THE YOUTH HOSTEL IN SHANGHAI
A very strange sex massage at Dingling sauna

Magna and Suzy Size boarded another one of those futuristic bullet trains in Hangzhou that took them to Shanghai in one hour and 18 minutes. The highest speed was 244 kilometres per hour. This form of transportation is so civilised! Not once during the whole trip did a train leave late. As soon as the train is on its way, polite attendants will offer you coffee, drinks and snacks. No beer, though.

The landscape flies by the windows and in no time you have reached another Huochezhan where you board one of those inexpensive taxis. Still young at heart, Suzy had chosen Shanghai Y 35, the Youth Hostel near People's Square, and had overcome the language barrier by taking a picture of the map on their website. The taxi driver at the train station took a close look at it and off they went.

At the reception of said Youth Hostel, your two travelling heroines were asked if they had a reservation. Since they did not, the friendly girl checked her books very carefully and finally decided that she could accommodate the two grey ladies.

As tempting as it might have been, they did not opt for the dormitory but for single rooms with their own bathrooms and wifi for the usual 180 Yuan (US$26). It would have been easy to bring new friends to the room, just pretending to take them for a drink at the bar on the third floor when passing the reception downstairs. But before you can smuggle someone in, you have to find him.

The Youth Hostels in China are not — as you probably would expect — for young people only, with rigid rules to keep the rough ones at bay. They all have quite inviting bars with pool tables and other interesting games and the one in Shanghai even had a 'Happy Hour' that lasted from 8pm to 10pm.

Magna — who drinks much less than Suzy — could have her daily Jameson with Coke as a nightcap there, if they made it home before

11pm when the bar closes. Admittedly, this did not happen all that often since Shanghai has, by far, the most open and vivid gay scene in all of China and the two discoverers worked many night shifts.

At the time of the visit, the first Shanghai Pride was held, but neither Suzy nor Magna were very interested in those events, they were clearly after close and personal contact. Call it sex, if you must.

It is always a bit difficult to find your way in a new Chinese city and Suzy therefore contacted Pan Tao, a 26-year-old Shanghai gay guide with appealing looks who offers his services on his website. But he had no time for your two heroines as other customers had hired him for a job.

Suzy had printed the Shanghai Gay Map (provided by Pan Tao) back in Castelgandolfo, which helped her and Magna find their way around.

Once they had found Eddys, which is the oldest gay bar in Shanghai, the rest was not really easy, but manageable. They were a bit early at Eddys and only a few guests had arrived. They started a conversation with another visitor, Frederick, a Chinese guy who lives in Australia together with his Farang boyfriend of many years.

He was interested in Suzy and later that night invited her to join him at his fancy hotel, but since he was a top as well and due to acute tiredness, she missed that tempting opportunity.

Shanghai Studio is more or less opposite Eddys and clearly more lively than the latter. It is located underground in an old, very spacious bunker that houses several bars and dance floors, as well as an art gallery. A young and cheerful crowd gathers here after 9pm till late, but neither Magna nor Suzy managed to make a catch.

They tried their luck the next day at Studio 2006, a fancy gay sauna that is also in a spacious underground bunker near Shanghai Studio. The entrance fee is relatively expensive (80 Yuan, about US$11.50) and most visitors were young and sporty beautiful people that were clearly not interested in meeting old Farang tarts. In a way it was interesting to visit that well-designed place, but since all those hunks knew how good-looking they were, they were all a bit conceited and it was thus a chaste visit.

Suzy and Magna also went to G Massage, where they have good-looking masseurs indeed, but they are really pricy, especially if you come from the gay heaven of good old Pattaya, so neither of your two stingy heroines got laid that night.

During the day they wandered around Shanghai, visiting the Bund and other places of interest. But after sunset, they developed their specific gay interests as usual.

The easiest gay place to find in Shanghai was Ding Lin Men Club, a sauna with some (affordable) massage boys. Just take Subway Number 1 to Yang Chan Road, leave through Exit 3 and walk for 800 metres on Yang Chan Road until you reach unit number 775.

It is a spacious sauna and not smelly as described by Pan Tao. In order to enter, you have to become a member (for 20 Yuan) and the entrance fee after is then 35 Yuan. Suzy had a short look in the steam room where someone gave someone else a blowjob, but she was not interested in those dirty old men. (Call them 'sexually active senior citizens' instead of dirty old men, if you want to be politically correct.)

She grabbed the best looking masseur she could find and went with him into the massage room after signing the bill for 180 Yuan. It was the strangest sex massage of her life. The masseur did not get undressed, and would not do anything except let your heroine touch his fast-swelling dick under his pants — he was not wearing any underwear. He looked constantly at the glass window in the door, pointing out that he would get fired if caught in the act (quite incredible in a gay sauna).

Suzy managed to come, but do not ask how, she must have been really desperate. Since it would have been an inconvenient train ride to Qingdao, they booked a flight which was — at 490 Yuan or US$70 — even cheaper than the train.

BIG FISH CAUGHT AT QINGDAO BAY
Where the Germans introduced beer to the Chinese

Arriving at yet another spick and span airport in Qingdao, the well-known Northern-Chinese port city, Suzy and her older sister Magna Size had to prove that they did not have a fever. Such is travel during the swine flu epidemic. But your two heroines passed the wary health officials in no time, grabbed their luggage and were on their way to the old part of town, located on a sort of peninsula facing the sea.

In 2008, Qingdao hosted the sailing competition of the Olympics. The airport is brand new and all the roads to the old centre of town are state of the art.

They had told the taxi driver to go to the Railway hotel, which was mentioned in the *Lonely Planet*. But the driver misunderstood them and took them to the historic railway station where they soon found another suitable hotel at a low price.

If you take the pain, fellow gay tourist, to check out the relevant Gay Guides for Asia, you will notice that there are no entries for scenic Qingdao. For once, your two well-travelled gay sentinels had no expectations at all when it came to encounters of a certain kind and no plans to corrupt the youth of yet another city. Still, they were looking forward to visiting that place.

But on the first day they could not see a thing, because of the thick and rather cold mist. Both your heroines thus retired early.

By the next morning the mist was gone and the sun was shining. From their hotel rooms they had a view of the old train station. In 1898, Kaiser Wilhelm II sent his troops into Qingdao when two German missionaries were murdered and they stayed on till 1914 when the Japanese took over.

There are many historic buildings and landmarks to be seen in Qingdao. You sometimes get the feeling of being in Bavaria or Hamburg, walking through the streets and enjoying the friendly atmosphere. Try fresh seafood or meat kebabs on offer all over the town, together with incredibly cheap local draught beer. It was the Germans who opened the famous Tsingtao (that is how Qingdao is pronounced) Brewery in 1903 and thus introduced beer to the Chinese, a very laudable deed.

Walk around the old town and enjoy the beauty of it. Suzy and Magna did just that, sometimes walking together, sometimes alone, only to bump into each other again. They visited several churches, people-watched, saw the different beaches and just enjoyed the place, which is most beautiful in summer.

But then a totally unexpected thing happened: lazy Suzy was sitting in a restaurant having a delicious dark beer when she saw Magna walk by on the other side of the street. Naturally, Suzy shouted at her unsuspecting older sister: "Maagna, Maaaagna!"

Magna is usually easily convinced to have a beer, since she just loves dark beer. But, as it turned out, she was currently not philandering alone. Earlier, when she had routinely inspected the public toilet at Qingdao bay — sanitation certainly is one of mankind's achievements — she had seen a very big fish there indeed.

The proprietor of said fish — a maybe 30-year-old Chinese — had followed her since like a puppy. Of course he was invited to join the two elder sisters for a beer. He could hardly speak any English and so the communication was a bit basic, but there was an advantage to that too.

Magna, who really does have a very good heart and proved to be a wonderful companion on countless occasions during their whole trip through China, suddenly asked Suzy if she wanted to take over her catch. He wasn't really her type; she preferred the girlish boys.

But still, that was such a nice and truly unexpected — one could even say noble — gesture that hardened Suzy Size was moved to tears. Of course, she asked Magna again and again, if this was really OK. When your heroine was absolutely assured that Magna could not care less, she invited the young and butch man to call on her quarters.

They passed the reception desk without the least problem; nobody minded the beginning of a long and beautiful Farang-Chinese friendship.

The fish rightly proved to be as big as Magna had earlier noted. The sex was great. But then he wanted money.

Suzy was a bit surprised at first; she just had not expected that. But then she handed him 200 Yuan (about US$29), a truly well spent amount. A little later, she walked him out of the hotel and out of her life.

BEIJING HAS CHANGED BEYOND RECOGNITION
A splendid young man at Destination

China, gay tourist, is at present an inexpensive country to travel to. Suzy did the math, and she spent about US$60 a day during her month-long trip, including absolutely everything, even the occasional boys.

After Beijing, Magna and Suzy took another overnight train to Xian where they visited the world famous terracotta soldiers — certainly the cultural highlight of the whole trip — before travelling to Kunming by plane. But these two legs (Xian and Kunming) proved to not be interesting, strictly from a gay point of view.

It is not that there are no gays, gay venues or cruisy parks to be found in these places. But Suzy and even Magna felt a bit tired and worn out, and just not in the mood to search for them, which can be an arduous task if your Chinese is rusty or non-existent. Both your heroines are spoilt by the ease of all such endeavours in good old Pattaya, too.

Besides, Suzy and Magna had by now grasped how to operate in China, which certainly was part of the goal of this educational trip — avoid the tempting, but expensive gay massage services, which often promise much more than they actually deliver. Visit bars or saunas or just trust your conventional gay senses.

Suzy will spare you the details of Xian and Kunming and concentrate on her wonderful time in Beijing in this chapter.

It was another top modern bullet train that brought your two gay sentinels from Qingdao to Beijing in 6 hours. Suzy cannot remember which one of the many train stations was their destination — there are four or five such stations in the Chinese capital.

Your two travelling heroines had booked Kelvin's Studio Apartments for 5 days. This friendly (gay) Chinese guy offers inexpensive studios with air conditioning, TV, a fridge, microwave, wireless internet and a bath with hot and cold shower in a central Beijing location.

Suzy and Magna flagged down a taxi in the direction of the New World Centre Shopping Mall, before calling Kelvin on the phone, who then gave the driver more detailed directions in Chinese.

He dropped the two grey sisters in front of a famous Beijing noodle shop called Noodle King, and Kelvin arrived in no time on a bicycle. Everything proved to be as advertised and after being paid, friendly Kelvin left Suzy and Magna with the magnetic key cards for the main entrances and an old-fashioned metal key for the room door. Although small, the room was absolutely fine and the location really was central (close to the old train station and not very far from Tiananmen Square) and fortunately very private, indeed.

Suzy had last been to Beijing about 15 years ago and was simply amazed by its incredible transformation. Of course she could remember the old train station and believes she even found the old hotel which she stayed in nearby, all those years ago. And the famous — or infamous — Tiananmen Square is still the same, but maybe even more strictly controlled than your heroine remembers. But besides that? About 90% of all motorcycles are now electric and, judging by their age, must have been driven by batteries for years. Compared to 15 years ago, the air is absolutely clear and much better than in Bangkok. Nobody spits on the floors any longer.

People are extremely kind and helpful, not rude as hell as before. (Maybe they were re-educated for the Olympics?) You see countless shopping centres all over, modern facilities, and consumerism blooming at an unabated speed. Suzy watched all those Chinese masses eating Big Macs, Kentucky Fried Chicken and all that horrible fast food in their typical outlets.

She had her — by now customary — Chinese breakfast at KFC, consisting of coffee and those little egg tarts. But as luck (or misfortune) would have it, a female tart (hooker) approached Suzy — or rather Fritzy Frizz — right there at KFC, drew your innocent maiden heroine into conversation and then offered to visit her at her private quarters, clearly having the private parts of Fritzy in mind. And then afterward, said vulgar woman would certainly have presented a bill for services not even desired at all and almost unspeakable for a honorable homosexual.

Even after that traumatic experience Suzy still had her breakfasts at KFC, but was extremely careful of whom to converse with in that Beijing vice den.

Aside from her Western breakfast, she preferred traditional Chinese food, and had a delicious beef noodle soup at Noodle King more than once or even Beijing duck when she was invited by an old friend to a typical Chinese feast at a restaurant. But, gay tourist to China, Suzy hears you asking, where is the meat?

Magna discovered it at a nearby park, where she made two catches, but could only drag one to her room. And he was too shy to be introduced to Suzy Size properly, so Suzy had to bank on Magna's most enthusiastic descriptions.

Suzy found her own Beijing destiny at Destination, which is the largest and most popular gay bar, disco and dance locale in the Chinese capital.

The minute your heroine entered, she could not help but notice a young man with a funny hat, who reminded her slightly of black American singer Billy Mo, when he performed his unforgettable song 'Ich kauf mir lieber einen Tirolerhut' (1962), which had been quite a hit back then in Germany.

Said young man laid eyes on your greying heroine right from the minute she entered. Suzy was of course flattered, but secretly wondered if there might something be wrong with his eyes. But, no, he really showed interest in your heroine, following her everywhere throughout the premises.

They soon started a conversation — he spoke English excellently — and only a little later they were sharing deep and passionate French kisses. They stayed close together at Destination for at least an hour; kissing, embracing, touching here and there or simply holding hands like teenagers.

Magna had made a catch herself and did more or less the same just beside them, but then decided to go home with her man. Suzy and her newly discovered prince charming had another beer and gin tonic respectively at lively Destination.

Suzy was so preoccupied with her love of the night on those inviting premises, that she forgot to inspect the upper floor for you, gay tourist to China... sorry, so very sorry, you have to do that yourself.

Then her new companion got hungry — a bit like the boys in Thailand. They went across the street to the fancy Bellagio late night restaurant, well after midnight. At least half the crowd was gay, and the waitresses with their short hair all looked like lesbians.

Suzy was finally allowed to pay the bill, after she overcame his strong resistance; the young man had his wallet out first. And then your old heroine and that fine lad finally went home.

He was 25 years old and stayed all night. He was just after older Farang men, not their money. Due to his haste in having to leave for work the next day, he forgot his watch. Another successful meeting was thus arranged a few hours before Suzy left Beijing.

KHOB CHAI (THANK YOU), MR. GOOD
An overland trip from Kunming to Luang Prabang

Suzy and Magna Size could have easily taken a flight from Kunming to Bangkok, thus ending their great gay China Friendship Tour. But, after looking at a map, they were tempted to go overland, which used to be difficult or even impossible just a few years back.

They decided to visit Laos (Luang Prabang), where Magna had never been before. Suzy had been to Luang Prabang at least 12 times, but did not mind returning. Your heroine loves that place for its stunning beauty, but not for the gay night life, though. She must admit: she never got laid in Luang Prabang, despite the many previous visits. But she might be lucky this time...

There was a very able travel agent just in front of the Camellia hotel where your two grey gay sentinels were staying at in Kunming. Suzy had wanted to stay at the Camellia for nostalgic reasons; she had stayed there on her last trip to China about 15 years ago.

And it proved to be a good choice: centrally located, inexpensive and gay-friendly as it would have been possible to bring 'hardware' to the room. One just needed to stop at the hotel bar first for a drink, thus deviating the attention of the reception girls.

The two elder ladies were at first a bit shocked when they heard that the bus ride from Kunming to Luang Prabang would take 30 hours. As you know, fellow gay tourist, neither Magna nor Suzy can be regarded as a spring chicken any longer. And sitting on a bus for 30 hours can be a bit long, even for younger travellers.

But after the travel agent explained that this was a sleeping bus, with beds allocated to all passengers, Suzy and Magna finally went for it.

To be sure not to starve to death on their long bus trip, they went to Carrefour in Kunming and bought all kinds of food. Suzy bought Chinese dried ham (a bit on the salty side), baguettes, cherries, peaches and Great Wall red wine, which is inexpensive and very drinkable. Magna opted for cheese, butter, cooked ham, onions and that horrible soft bread the English and Americans like so much.

The bus was quite comfortable in the beginning, and it left very punctually in the late afternoon. For several hours, your two heroines watched the interesting landscape fly by outside the windows. The roads seemed to be brand new, as so many others they had seen in China.

The only problem was, they had no toilet on board. Every few hours, the bus would stop somewhere for a break and the facilities were very basic, to put it mildly. After a longer ride without stopping, everybody rushed to the toilets and it must have been then when Suzy's laptop, which was stored under her bed on the floor of the bus, got stolen. Your heroine only realised this the next morning when they were at the border to Laos, but it would have been useless to make a fuss.

To cross over into Laos proved to be a bit difficult, due the painstakingly slow ways of the Lao immigration personnel. PDR is the acronym for Peoples Democratic Republic of Laos, but it is often translated as 'Please Don't Rush'. It took them no less than five hours to process the Chinese bus.

There was considerable discussion between the Chinese bus people and the Lao immigration personnel on how to tax certain parcels the Chinese had with them. Suzy thinks the bus might have been operated by the Chinese Secret Service...

After that delay at the border, that bus ride seemed to get longer and longer, and the roads in Laos were not as good as in China. Your two heroines felt worn out and tired when they finally arrived in Luang Prabang after 29 hours.

Apparently the procedure at the border crossing always takes a lot of time, since they arrived one hour before schedule. Would they take that bus ride again? No, probably not.

The *tuk tuk* driver brought them to Sokdee Guest House, which was nice accommodation and one of the reception boys instantly wanted to 'take care' of Suzy in an unambiguous way.

It is pure pleasure to walk through that beautiful and well-preserved town which clearly deserves its status as a World Heritage Site. There are many good and inexpensive restaurants; Suzy and Magna both tried a tasty water buffalo steak at Café de Paris and were very happy with that choice.

Magna once again had taken the initiative and asked a *tuk tuk* driver to bring your two heroines to the most prominent gay bar in Luang Prabang. He dropped them at Khob Chai, which indeed seemed to be gay-centric, judging from the staff.

They chatted with another customer who happened to live in Luang Prabang. He told them that Khob Chai had indeed been an openly gay bar with drag shows until the authorities made a big fuss a while ago. The US owner and his Lao partner then turned it into a 'straight' bar like their other joint just across the street, which is called Lao Lao Garden.

But despite this official change of sexual orientation, Khob Chai is the obvious choice to search for local talent in Luang Prabang. A 19-year-old waiter, Mr. Good, got friendly with Suzy and they arranged to go to Dao Fai Disco the next evening after Khob Chai closed. Magna, who had also made such an acquaintance, joined them.

The grey ladies did not have too good a time at the noisy disco, but their subsidised new friends had, which was the main objective of that visit and therefore fine.

The usual hunger after the disco had to be fought with a noodle soup at the only late night restaurant in Luang Prabang. And when it closed — rather early, Suzy could finally get rid of her unwanted Luang Prabang chastity.

Thank you, Mr. Good, thank you very, very big!

Magna took a plane to Bangkok two days later and Suzy returned via bus and Vientiane to Nong Khai and her residence there. Then she returned to good old Pattaya, where the living is so incredibly easy.

BOBBY
Thailand

09

MY BOBBY IS OVER THE OCEAN
Eulogy for the best friend

Tragedy had struck at Castelgandolfo. Emptiness could be sensed inside the house and out in the lush gardens. It felt as if the sun stopped shining, the birds stopped singing and the world stopped turning when Khun Amorn, the boyfriend of your heroine, unceremoniously delivered the bad news to Suzy Size, while she was repotting some of her precious plants.

"Bobby has died already."

Bobby is dead? Bobby, the best friend of Suzy Size? How can that be? Why? Why? Why?

When hearing about the death of someone else, one immediately thinks of their own mortality. Death is always unexpected. Did not your heroine's insurance agent die out of the blue just the other week? Well, he seemed to drink too much.

But beloved Bobby did not adhere to this vice. OK, he liked a good fuck, when he could get one... but that is nothing strange to the male psyche. And Bobby was not really sick. Occasional nose bleeding lately, that was all.

Bobby never betrayed your heroine, unlike all the other boys of Pattaya or Asia. He was the truest of friends. He will be sadly missed and fondly be remembered. R.I.P.

When Bobby first arrived, he seemed to be in drag. When Suzy

Size awoke that happy morning, she saw what seemed to be a fair girl on her sunny terrace, and asked Khun Amorn, "What is Lilly doing on the terrace?"

He answered, "Lilly is in front of the house." And, truly, there she was. But who was Lilly's twin on the terrace?

Oh, 'she' was actually a male... another Golden Retriever had joined the family. To match the double 'L's in Lilly's name, Suzy named him Bobby, for its double 'B's. Only later did Suzy Size realise that Bobby had a dark side. He was a murderer.

A Thai policeman not far away had owned that wonderful Golden Retriever. But he had expensive fighting cocks as well. And Bobby had killed one of his precious fighting cocks.

Then the policeman beat Bobby terribly, almost killing him. Bobby ran away and took refuge in your heroine's garden. He was fed, and joined the gang as a welcome addition.

Well, he was not popular with the cocks and chickens in the neighbourhood. Whenever one of them accidentally entered his territory, they would not live for long. And he had an aversion towards cats as well.

Suzy tried to keep her first cat on the other side of the house, which is separated from the dog area by a fence, but unfortunate Champa was torn apart when she walked into the dogs' grounds — all 4 of them were cat haters.

Then Suzy had to get rid of Bambi, a pincher. Bambi was a terribly dominant and jealous female. She bit Lilly, who was three times her size, all the time. When she bit Lilly so badly that the well-mannered

Golden Retriever went ballistic and would have killed Bambi, Bambi was sent to Nong Khai. But terrible Bambi also misbehaved badly there and was finally sent over to Laos... they eat canines in Laos.

Three dogs remained: Stefan, Lilly and Bobby. They successfully killed Suzy's two new cats when she was on her last grand voyage through Gay Asia.

And now Bobby has died. He was buried in the garden. But beware, cats! Stefan, a local Thai dog, quite close to a wolf, is still in place. He has taken over the reigns from Bobby, and he is now in charge. Stefan is an excellent watchdog, very alert.

Suzy Size has to wait until Lilly and Stefan follow poor Bobby to heaven before she can keep dogs and cats together. She will then get kittens and puppies at the same time. They will grow up without the old resentment between dogs and cats, and without old biases, they may even become friends.

The goal is to achieve some harmony in diversity, like in the real world. Get the rainbow flag up.

And that, is the opportunity of tragedy.

GOLDEN HORN ISTANBUL
Turkey

10

BLOWING A GOLDEN HORN IN ISTANBUL
How your heroine became a victim of Ramadan

After arriving in Istanbul, Suzy Size immediately gave Yuksel a call. He was supposed to meet your heroine the next day in Taksim Square. But neither of the two queens knew how the other looked like, since they only had exchanged emails so far.

Suzy described herself over the phone: 53 years old, greying, average type, definitely not younger looking than she really is, nice teeth (mostly false, of course), slightly too fat (too much beer) — but not so fat that her doctor recommends a diet, wearing short pants and carrying a backpack with a small umbrella... Suzy is definitely a prudent Swiss.

Standing in front of the Guaranti Bank the next day, next to the Marmara Hotel on Taksim square — too early as always — Suzy checked out all the males there. But none of them showed any signs of being Yuksel, nobody returned your heroine's expectant gaze.

When a good-looking young guy with a killer smile finally arrived, there was no doubt, this had to be Yuksel! They hugged each other warmly.

Travelling through Gay Asia is not always easy for your heroine, nor is it always interesting or rewarding. There are a lot of boring places and a lot of gay assholes out there. But Suzy is compensated by highlights — like meeting wonderful Yuksel, with his sensational smile, in Taksim square. Whenever Suzy looked at Yuksel during their conversations, she would start to smile too, since his smile is so highly contagious. Suzy must have looked a lot like Malvolio in Shakespeare's *Twelfth Night*.

Yuksel is the owner of Istanbul Queens, an internet-based gay guide for Istanbul. The two queens had some coffee at a friendly café on Istikal Road, which is the main shopping street in Istanbul. Most gay bars are within walking distance from Taksim Square and the famous Istikal Road. Actually, most of the nightlife in Istanbul is located in the small streets around Istikal Road.

While talking to wonderful Yuksel, Suzy tried to find out if he might be interested in elder men like her. But, alas, he was living together with his boyfriend of about the same age, both working in the hotel industry. Suzy was a bit heartbroken, but showed a brave face as usual, the show must go on!

Did their parents know about their sexual orientation? No, they kept quiet. The parents might know or suspect, but by not telling (and not asking), all parties involved kept their face.

The gay nightlife in Istanbul is very vibrant; probably the most vibrant of any Muslim country (except Malaysia), but you do not openly wave the gay flag in the face of a still very conservative society.

Yuksel was expecting the visit of a younger cousin that evening, who had recently confided to the slightly older cousin that he was gay.

Before leaving for a friend's wedding preparations — the Turks are almost as wedding crazy as the Indians — Yuksel took your heroine by her hand and walked her to some gay bars nearby, to save her some time.

Your heroine invited Yuksel and his husband (or wife?) to stay at her

Castelgandolfo residence, if the two splendid young men should ever make it to Thailand. As an old and motherly queen it is sometimes so pleasant to have gorgeous young men around, even if it leads to no sexual action, only a smile and maybe a hug.

The gay nightlife in Istanbul starts late, so it is completely useless to go to a bar early. Suzy started her journey around 11pm at Otherside (which is on the third floor of a building more or less opposite the McDonald's on Taksim square), but there was hardly anybody there initially. There was no entrance fee, but a beer did cost 10 Lira (US$1 is equal to 1.50 Lira).

Tek Yon (which means: 'one way') is a large disco, on weekends they charge 12 Lira as an entrance fee which includes a drink. After midnight there was a sizeable crowd, although only a few were dancing. Since it is illegal nowadays to smoke in restaurants, bars and discos in Turkey, Tek Yon has covered about half of their large courtyard with a roof and at times more people seemed to be out there instead of on the dance floor. Suzy Size has never been a dancer, but likes to watch the young and hip doing it. Although that hardly ever leads to anything but a little voyeurism. One beer later, your heroine left in the direction of Sahara bar, but never made it there.

Sahara charges 20 Lira for its entrance fee and is located in the same alley as Aquarius. It is supposed to have many money boys, which is admittedly attractive for your heroine. Suzy had contemplated taking a tasty Turk from Sahara and going with him to Aquarius sauna, which is open 24 hours a day. Under no circumstances would she take one of them to her hotel room, it was far too dangerous.

Walking up Sadri Alisik Sokak road, she suddenly saw the sign for Deja Vu bar — which was not a déjà vu. How many times had she passed here in search of Deja Vu, but just could not find it? Now, at night, the sign was fully lit and that made the difference, Deja Vu could finally been seen amongst the other signs.

Deja Vu charges 10 Lira (includes a drink) as an entrance fee and is, like Sahara, a place where older men meet hustlers. Suzy only liked one of them, but he was more interested in a local big shot. Another one of the boys — who was dancing without a T-shirt — was so drunk, he could hardly stand. He helped himself uninvited to the drinks of other guests, and was pushed around until the management threw him out to the street. Suzy had seen enough of that slightly crazy scene and left thereafter.

Even in the early hours of the morning there still were many people drinking, singing and partying in the streets around Istikal. Nightlife in Istanbul does not stop before 5am, even during Ramadan — and now, gay tourist to Turkey, the really interesting part of this Istanbul account follows.

Suzy Size is always amazed by how professionally the touts in Istanbul work. You can hardly pass a restaurant in the tourist areas without being approached by one of those multilingual employees who will try to explain to you why you should have food or at least a drink at their outlet. They do a very good job and your heroine is easily convinced, she has given in to many of them. But surprisingly, while Suzy was walking by the many fish restaurants under Galata bridge, facing the famous Golden Horn and the Bosporus, no one approached her.

But they had a very cute waiter at one particular restaurant and

Suzy ordered a beer from him, not knowing that it was the first day of Ramadan. Since Istanbul is liberal when it comes to alcohol, her delicious Efes beer arrived in no time and Suzy engaged the cute waiter in conversation.

Abidin — which means slave to religion — is not his real name, but Suzy will call him so. He was 23 years old and had come from the impoverished Southeast of Turkey to Istanbul for work. There were 11 children in his family, and two of his brothers were working in other restaurants under the Galata bridge.

Abidin soon figured out that Suzy was gay and wrote his name and cell phone number on a piece of paper, which he handed to your heroine very discreetly — his colleagues are watchful. He told Suzy to call him after 8pm and that is what your horny heroine did.

When Suzy called him, Abidin said he would be free at 9.30pm and then they "could go somewhere". He did not want to meet her at the restaurant (being aware of his colleagues or his brothers and others talking), so they met opposite the Galata bridge, at the entrance of New Mosque — which is not very new actually, it was built between 1597 and 1663. There is a little park with benches just behind New Mosque, which is located at the foot of the Golden Horn; it is very busy during the day.

Abidin hugged Suzy when she arrived, not unlike Yuksel had done, but much more intensely. He led your heroine to those now-empty park benches behind New Mosque where they first held hands, always aware that the garbage men were not too far away, removing the day's refuse. Then he hugged your heroine again, it felt great.

Suzy, who was always watching the garbage men out of the

corners of her eyes, wondered where they would end up. Abidin, who was obviously gay, knew of a convenient short time hotel nearby for the time after the prelude.

He was now working on the tits of your heroine, squeezing the nipples forcefully. Then he asked Suzy to lie on the bench, putting her head on his lap. He put three of his fingers in and out of her mouth, obviously knowing what he was doing. Suzy Size felt like Deep Throat. Then he unbuttoned his fly and a big hard cock emerged, as erect as the famous Galata Tower on the other side of the bridge.

Suzy stopped watching the garbage men nearby and started sucking that great cock. But then Abidin put it back into his pants. Today was the first day of Ramadan.

Abidin had served food and beer to his guests at the restaurant, but had himself obeyed the Muslim rules of fasting all day. Gay sex was always forbidden by his religion, but seemed to be an even bigger sin to Abidin during Ramadan.

During Ramadan, the devil is chained, therefore the 'bad things' that you do come from you alone. Abidin would have loved to have sex with Suzy, but not during Ramadan.

They stayed on that bench and played around for a long time. That tasty Turk took out his golden horn again and again, but always stopped short when he was approaching an orgasm. He tried to sodomize Suzy with his finger, but was stopped by your heroine, who explained that she was a top.

In Abidin's eyes, Suzy was not gay if she would not be fucked. And Abidin saw himself not as homo- or even bisexual, but as a completely straight guy who wanted to get married later when he had earned enough money, and have only three children, unlike his parents who had eleven.

Abidin begged Suzy to come back to Istanbul after Ramadan and have sex with him, since he was very horny all the time. All young men are always horny all the time.

And Suzy Size, remembering that intense night when she became a victim of Ramadan, is certainly inclined to accede to Abidin's desire and to return to the wonderful Golden Horn as soon as possible.

ABIDIN, MON AMOUR!
Istanbul can be cold at times

Suzy Size was looking forward to returning to Istanbul. She was absolutely fascinated by this great, historic city at the Bosporus, which was vibrant and good fun in every possible respect.

She had made contact again with lovely and young Yuksel. She wanted to invite him and his (so far) unknown boyfriend for dinner: for old queens it can be delightful just being surrounded by nice, good-looking gay men, even though sex is out of the question.

The chemical industry has so far managed to take care of erectile dysfunction, but a real achievement would be a pill that makes young and horny men fall instantly in love with old tarts. How easily could such a wonder drug clandestinely be dropped in a drink of an adored young man, but alas, there are obvious limits to the abilities of the darn chemical industry.

Your heroine loves the incredible Spice Market near New Mosque in Istanbul and went there to buy a kilogramme of olives, vacuumed in order to last without refrigeration throughout the ten days in Egypt before she was to return to Thailand. She roamed the streets once again, but Istanbul was now (around Easter) terribly cold. Suzy was wearing a shirt, a pullover and a jumper — even socks, which she hates so much.

In the summer time, when the living is easy, there are numerous salesmen around Istanbul selling corn cobs, either boiled or grilled. Now, Suzy noticed all the chestnut sellers as a sign of the cooler season.

The main reason why Suzy Size had returned to lovely Istanbul was Abidin. He had begged Suzy to come back to Istanbul after Ramadan and have sex with him, since he was very horny all the time. And now good old Suzy was back.

Naturally, your heroine called that splendid young man the minute she arrived in Istanbul, but some silly woman who could not speak a word of English answered. She did not seem to know adorable Abidin, even though your heroine repeated that beloved name again and again.

In her growing despair, Suzy tried the number several times, but to no avail. If only she had one of those lamps that Aladdin had, to ask a genie to look up Abidin's phone number or carry the guy himself into the arms of your horny heroine!

In haste, Suzy went to Galata Bridge, where Abidin used to work as a waiter. But now during the off-season, there were few guests and even fewer waiters at those restaurants that were so popular in summer. No trace of Abidin could be found.

Suzy mourned her loss. She went back to that empty park bench behind New Mosque and probably would have lit a candle or two if she had any religious bone in her body. She would have laid down dozens of red roses, if only it would have helped.

Whatever happened to Abidin, Suzy may never know. Was he just sacked because of low season, and expected to return in due time? Did he run into a nest of snakes and get fatally bitten on his heel? If so, your loving heroine would climb down to Hades in an instant and try to get him out with her heavenly music. Unfortunately, this would not work either, since Suzy Size (unlike Orpheus) has no musical talent at all. Thus, tragically, ended this visit to Istanbul.

Needless to say, your shaken heroine did not even call Yuksel and have him and his boyfriend over for dinner. She was in no mood for conversation; she just could not bear any human company.

And the olives she bought in Spice Market were all spoilt upon her arrival in Thailand. There was a hole in the plastic bag. The vacuum was gone, the damage done.

GAY CHIANG MAI REVISTED
Thailand

11

SECRETS AND DREAMS REVEALED DURING DRUNKEN NIGHTS

Suzy Size had a splendid time when revisiting Chiang Mai. The scene had blossomed greatly in the last few years.

A new gay hotel called Lavender Lanna had recently opened. It was advertised everywhere and caused quite a media hype within the gay community. It was supposed to be the biggest gay hotel in the world.

Lavender Lanna was located in the building that used to be Tokyo Hotel, right around the corner of Central Kad Suan Kaew shopping centre. Most gay places in the city are located within this area (or not too far away). They had upgraded, renovated and redesigned the whole place, which now has more than 100 rooms. They offered a number of facilities, including a 24-hour lobby restaurant, a lobby bar, a 24-hour gift shop, a swimming pool with a pool bar and poolside massage and salon services available, and the Lavender Lanna Salon and Massage. They had also opened Power Boys, a glitzy show bar and nightclub in the basement. About 90% of their staff was supposed to be gay, but of course straight guests were allowed in as well, if they behaved properly.

Suzy Size has seen many gay institutions all over the world, but never any that big. And size, as you must know by now, matters to your benign heroine.

But the whole venture was a big failure. Suzy had a so-called massage at their premises and it was one of the worst in her life. The service at the various outlets was substandard. Guests complained about a wide range of issues on the relevant internet forums: there were only negative and very negative comments.

And when the American owner committed suicide not much later, the whole operation failed miserably. There were rumours he was poisoned, but nobody seems to know the truth. But the huge gay hotel is gone now; it was probably too big for somewhat laidback Chiang Mai.

After the lousy massage at Lavender Lanna, Suzy checked out her other options on the internet the next day. Was she going to try out River House Massage? It looked tempting. Or perhaps any of the others?

Since Suzy was walking near Classic House that fair afternoon, she decided to give it another try. Never change a winning horse; your heroine had been here before and emerged very satisfied.

The friendly receptionist explained the procedure: one hour of oil massage is 500 Baht, and the minimum tip is 600 Baht. Then you can pick a young man from the album, for instance Mr. Sak (24), who is a bottom.

Then you go upstairs, take a shower and lay down in the room. There is a mattress on the wooden floor and the procedure takes its course. Needless to say, Mr. Sak got more than the minimum tip. He chose the right job, enjoying his hard work very, very visibly. He must get a thrill out of the situation. Sitting there, waiting for an unknown Farang to come. Then that Farang will choose him, which is a narcissistic excitement. And then playing the game that he obviously enjoys. One cannot fake this.

And in the end, he gets paid the equivalent of four or five times the daily minimum wage. When your heroine came to Chiang Mai the very first time in 1982, there was just one (empty) gay bar that offered to call in some boys, but shy Suzy (back then) refused the friendly offer.

She might have been a bit like Johan, the cute young Dutch intern of Lavender Lanna she got to know at Soho bar and guesthouse, where she was staying this time around.

She met somewhat shy Johan again at breakfast the next day, at Amazing Sandwich next door. And again during an early drink at Soho bar. She bumped into Johan again and again, as well as the other guys who hung out at Soho bar. The melancholic Canadian, the funny Swede, the straight American couple that just loved that cheerful gay bar.

Having said all this, while the Chiang Mai gay scene has grown a lot lately, it still consists of a small, compact crowd and you see familiar faces everywhere. And with all these familiar faces you will not get lost, everybody knows everybody and most are on friendly terms with one another. And gossiping is the greatest pastime on earth.

Suzy went to see the famous show at Adams Apple — yes, this legendary Chiang Mai gay bar has reopened at its old premises, but has been completely redesigned. The show is very good, sleazy like in the old days. Many hunks were recruited, and they show it all. If, like your heroine, you believe in size, you are certainly at the right place here.

But the favourite hangout (headquarters) of your heroine in gay Chiang Mai was still Soho. The rooms are inexpensive, but have all the amenities you need in a very central location, just within walking distance from many gay places. And you just have to walk downstairs to sit in your heroine's favourite bar.

Scott, the American owner, is an excellent host; both funny and discreet at the same time. He will talk to you if you want to talk and leave you alone if you want to be left alone. He can sense that. His able Thai staff are friendly and attentive, too. Tan was your heroine's favourite... unreachable Tan, Suzy fancied him so much.

Suzy heard a lot of stories while sitting at Soho bar in Chiang Mai, she listens well and does not get drunk easily, whereas the beers loosen up her victims, and make them reveal their darkest or well-kept secrets.

One guy told her about his coming out in Pattaya. Another confessed not to have had sex in nine months. He had been fucked by such a big cock once that he got severely hurt in the process. But now he secretly fancied waiter Tan — who does not? — and would love to restart his sex life with him.

Yet another guy told Suzy about his intensive death wish for his mother. The woman is filthy rich, but would disinherit him if she knew he was gay. Understandably, he wishes her to be dead.

Suzy thinks this is a very common wish. Parents are always parents and many children want to get rid of them eventually. Maybe not today, but the day after tomorrow would suit just fine.

The drunken nights at Soho are very revealing.

LOVE TRAGEDIES AND COMEDIES
Sri Lanka

12

A LOVE TRAGEDY IN COLOMBO
The merciless trains leave too punctually in Sri Lanka

Imagine this: Suzy Size is sitting in the only first class compartment of a Kandy-bound train in the Colombo Fort Station. Beside her in the isle seat is Magna Size, her older sister, who does not yet sense the tragic events about to unfold.

In the row in front of your heroine are Khun Amorn, your heroine's Thai boyfriend of so many years and Khun Sun, Magna's heartthrob.

Mr. Iflar, a gay Sri Lankan man, had just passed by the open window outside and discreetly handed a neatly folded piece of paper to your stunned heroine. Beside his phone number, the note contained an unmistakable message: "I love you." It was written on the back of an ATM receipt from "Mamanella Branch", wherever this bank may be.

But alas, time had run out, and the merciless train left punctually at 3.35pm as scheduled. Suzy Size waved discreetly back at a devastated Mr. Iflar who looked sad, incredibly sad.

It was raining a little. The sky must have been sad as well.

Two days earlier, the party of four had landed at the airport in Colombo at around midnight, from Bangkok. A taxi brought them to the famous Galle Face Hotel, which was founded in the middle of the 19th century. They had booked inexpensive double rooms (without a view) for US$63. Where in the world can you live in colonial splendor for that kind of money?

If you cannot stay there, fellow gay tourist to Sri Lanka, just visit this unique hotel from a bygone time for a drink at the terrace or enjoy a buffet lunch, dinner or high tea.

The 26-year civil war — which prevented or hindered almost all economic development and thus preserved places like the Galle Face Hotel with its slightly worn-out charm — ended in March of 2009, when the government brutally wiped out the Tamil Tigers. But Colombo is still as if it were under siege. There are military control posts all over the city; after all, there were many bomb attacks in the past. Colombo is not a beautiful place. There are some old Colonial buildings, but you do not want to walk around much.

But on the first day they tried just that. Being European, Suzy and Magna love to walk whereas Khun Amorn and Khun Sun, typical of Thais, are strongly opposed to any such weird undertakings.

One could catch a suntan! (And therefore look like a poor farmer boy.) Or one might sweat! (And then smell like a bird shit Farang.) And one will certainly get very, very tired! (And thus have to retire from the beloved loud and very late disco far too early.)

They headed for the Fort Train Station to look for a train to Kandy. You may have heard, gay tourist to Asia, that they have a tooth of Lord Buddha at the temple in Kandy.

It was this very tooth that got Khun Amorn interested in a trip to a strange place like Sri Lanka. Khun Sun was very skeptical and hesitant at first, but finally agreed to leave the safe grounds of Thailand for a dubious land like Sri Lanka when he heard about the casinos in Colombo. But he would probably not be fooled again, since the Stardust Casino lacked all star quality when visited, and was certainly not up to the very high standards of this distinguished Isarn country boy.

Walking the streets of Colombo in search of Fort Train Station, all the Sri Lankan men turned to look at Khun Amorn and Khun Sun, leaving Suzy and Magna Size bitterly unattended to. They all knew exactly what those two Thais represented.

In a land where homosexuality is illegal — that silly law was imposed by the British — but bisexuality is more or less the norm among younger men (although not spoken of), our two friends were very bold and flamboyant indeed.

The show went on street by street, one head turning after another, but needless to say, your four brave sentinels to gay Sri Lanka never reached that Fort Train Station by foot — they lost their way and took a *tuk tuk* in the end.

At the train station, they bought four first class tickets for the next day at 400 Rupees each (about US$4). The three-hour ride is very scenic, the most scenic train ride your heroine knows of in Asia.

As usual, Suzy and her funny group arrived early at the train station the next day. When the train arrived, they took their reserved seats in the non air-conditioned section. Khun Amorn and Khun Sun were seated right in front of the panoramic window, and the two Farangs in the row behind them.

When Magna came back into the car after a last smoke, Suzy asked her elder sister to check on her many bags containing all the high heels, frocks and fur coats (it can get kind of cold in Kandy). The train was going to leave in a little while and Suzy wanted to have a pee.

When your benign heroine entered the toilet, a very fat and ugly guy with a beard pointed out a place for her. Suzy had started to pee when the face of said man appeared on the other side through a little window separating the two urinals. He stared at your heroine's cock, his tongue making wild movements between his lips and he was obviously jerking off. Well, beauty certainly lies in the eye of the beholder.

When Suzy was safely back in her train seat, the ugly guy was standing at the wall opposite her window. He tried to make eye contact all the time. Then he wrote something on a piece of paper.

Suzy pointed to Khun Amorn in front of her, conveying that she was with somebody, using her boyfriend as a shield against these totally unwanted attempts at getting to know her. But the lovesick man just came over and discreetly slipped the piece of paper into Suzy's hand. Not even Magna noticed.

When Suzy read the mysterious message of Mr. Iflar, it read: "I love you. I like fuck with you." Suzy had sort of sensed that. Of course, your heroine felt pity for Mr. Iflar, who found your greying heroine so sensational. But what could she do? He was not her type at all.

The minutes till the train was to leave felt like an eternity. When it finally started to move, Suzy was so glad she was safely on her way to Kandy.

INSULTS IN KANDY

After arriving at Kandy train station — even the two Thais Khun Amorn and Khun Sun had enjoyed the scenic ride up the mountains, despite the fact that there was no air conditioning — the party of four queens naturally wanted to stay at Queens Hotel right across the lake and the famous temple with the tooth of Lord Buddha.

They were offered an air-conditioned room at US$50 a night, but tried US$40 as a counter offer. When Suzy was here last year, that was the rate she paid then. But this was not accepted now. They compromised at US$45, but only for one night. After that they had to move to a non air-conditioned room for US$40. Since it was quite cool in Kandy, this did not matter at all, except to the Thais, who lost a bit of face, but not that much to get upset about.

They now have a KFC and Pizza Hut in Kandy and quite a lot of tourists compared to the year before, when Suzy Size was virtually the only Farang around. An American tour group was staying at the Queens as well; loud and vulgar as expected of such straight brutes.

Early the next morning, Suzy Size and Khun Amorn walked around the Kandy lake, which does not take more than an hour.

Normally, Khun Amorn (like most Thais) would not participate in such an arduous endeavour. Why walk at all, if there are *tuk tuks*, taxis or other comfortable means of transportation?

But in cool Kandy, Khun Amorn was interested in experiencing the nature beside the famous temple. They spotted giant bats napping in the trees around the lake, thousands of big, fat fish that are regularly fed by Buddhist visitors to Kandy. There were several scary-looking, but harmless lizards in the lake — in Thailand their presence would be a sign of bad luck, but not so in Sri Lanka — and many apes running around and enjoying life. But after an hour, back at the Queens, groggy

Khun Amorn called it a day (more or less) and retired to their private quarters for a while.

Whenever the four friends roamed the streets of Kandy, nobody took notice of Magna and Suzy Size. The two Thais, obviously gay and giggling much of the day, once again stole the limelight. The male youth of Kandy adored the two Thai queens with their obvious star quality.

And surprisingly, the Thais enjoyed flirting with everyone, too. Suzy Size had expected them to be snobbish and to act cool. After all, those Sri Lankans were terribly dark, almost as black as the negros of Africa, so to speak, which is, after all, contrary to the Thai ideal of fair-skinned beauty. But no inhibitions were shown at all.

They also treated the staff at the hotel as equals, as brothers and sisters as if they were back in Thailand, asking all kinds of very direct and indiscreet questions: "How much do you earn a month?" And were amazed when they answered 6,000 Rupees, which amounts to about US$60. What? For a whole month?

They were also shocked to discover that there was no disco or shopping centre in this holy town, where every Sri Lankan is expected to pray at least once in his or her life at the tooth temple. Unbelievably, the very few bars in Kandy close at 11pm! What a very strange place, what a very strange country, indeed!

Our two naïve Thai friends were at friendly terms with every tout and bugger. There are many in Sri Lanka and some are refined, using any pretext to draw anybody into a conversation, then eventually try to sell you some rubbish, get some commission, or any form of money. "Some coins of your country, maybe?" The worst and most expensive ones are those who explain to you from the start that they do not want any money.

Look, fellow gay tourist to Sri Lanka, your heroine understands that there are many poor people in the country that need to make a living, but sometimes they get on her nerves anyhow.

And when another one, a nerdish ugly one, approached Khun Amorn and explained that he worked as a gardener at their hotel, Suzy asked, what hotel was this? When he did not know the answer, Suzy told him to get lost.

He got angry. "Who are you, to talk to me that way? That is very dangerous. You do not know who I am. You are a homosexual that likes to fuck young Thai boys."

The whole thing was a bit ridiculous, since Khun Amorn at 40 plus is far from being a young Thai boy. But the sudden homophobic outburst was still a telling and nasty thing. Both Magna and Suzy warned their Thai companions to be a bit more careful, not to act too obviously gay. And they finally convinced them not to buy beer for the 18-year-old acquaintances they had made at the hotel — in a holy city where the legal drinking age is 21. They seemed to abide by the rules.

But later on in the trip, after another catch in Nuwara Eliya, Khun Amorn confessed to having caught two fish while in Kandy.

Magna and Suzy should have known, after all the Thais had received and sent endless text messages to their many new Sri Lankan friends, had endless silly conversations on the mobile phone with a local sim card, and invited their catches to visit them in Thailand, not realising that they were expected to pay for their air fare!

OF NOSES AND YOUTH
Cold and hot nights in Nuwara Eliya

To move on from Kandy to Nuwara Eliya, Suzy and Magna Size decided to hire a van and driver. There were many van drivers in the streets of Kandy offering their services to tourists. The two bargain-savvy Farang travellers compared the offers they got and finally went for Mr. Samantha. This good-looking man had priced the two-day trip to Nuwara Eliya and an additional day to Hikkaduwa at 13,500 Rupees (about US$130), which was the best price.

But Suzy had a hidden agenda as well. She adored that butch guy with his beautiful smile and was secretly hoping for services other than just the driving. The drivers normally get a free small room at the chosen hotel, which might lead to nightly encounters of some sort.

Suzy called Mr. Samantha to convey the good news that he had gotten the job. "Give me 300," Mr. Samantha said on the phone. Suzy Size rushed back to the place where they had first met lovely Mr. Samantha to lock in him and his priceless services with that very low downpayment.

But when your heroine arrived, he actually wanted 3,000 Rupees to buy petrol (which was reasonable), and Suzy handed over that amount without getting a receipt. Then your heroine asked Mr. Samantha if he was married. He was and had two daughters already.

But this was no discouraging news. Most young men in Sri Lanka — married or not — are eager to play along as long as they can maintain their sexual identity. This means that they usually are willing to fuck you or will agree to receive a blowjob, but not the other way around. Some might kiss, but many will not adhere to such unmanly conduct.

But, alas, there was no Mr. Samantha at the Queens Hotel at the time agreed upon the next morning. Suzy tried to call him, but he would not answer. Had the hunk run away with the down payment?

Suzy was a bit worried, feeling stupid to not have insisted on a receipt, blinded instead by the good looks of this now so obviously fraudulent Mr. Samantha. But then he called back and said he would arrive soon. As it turned out, there was some sort of petrol crisis that day.

Perhaps supply was short? Maybe there had been a strike? It was not really clear, but there were extremely long queues at all petrol stations they passed during their drive up the hills to Nuwara Eliya. When he neared a queue that was relatively short, Mr Samantha pulled in and asked for 400 Rupees (but meant 4,000) to fill his gas tank.

The drive up from Kandy to Nuwara Eliya is very scenic and nice. The winding roads pass by endless tea fields and water falls and the altitude goes up from roughly 500 metres above sea level to almost 1,900 metres. With your own private vehicle you can stop wherever you please, take pictures or have tea plus a piece of the famous chocolate cake at one of the many tea factories.

Mr. Samantha proved to be an excellent and careful driver along that sometimes treacherous mountainous terrain full of crazy people at the wheels. He stopped whenever he was requested to and additionally proposed to drive to Hakgala Gardens (which dates back to 1861) after arriving in Nuwara Eliya.

The four friends stayed at Grosvenor Hotel, which is located in an old Colonial building, formerly the residence of the governor. They could get two double rooms at 3,000 Rupees (roughly US$30), which were spacious, had a fireplace and hot water in the bathroom. Hot water is essential, since the nights can get chilly up in those Sri Lankan mountains and you do not want to shower with cold water.

After philandering through the pleasant little town, the two Thai companions returned to the Grosvenor Hotel where they conducted endless talks with the young employees.

Suzy and Magna had a look at the unique Hill Club. Suzy had stayed there once, about 25 years ago. In order to be allowed as a guest, one had to become temporary member. At dinner, one was not allowed into the dining room without a jacket and tie, both of which could be rented for a small fee.

There were other odd rules and regulations that made the stay unforgettable. When Suzy and Magna enquired about vacancies at the lobby, they were told they could get a room for US$100 a night (compared to US$20 25 years ago) and all the old-fashioned rules were still in place. When they asked to have a look at the premises, they were denied that privilege due to Magna's sloppy short pants.

It was a miserable evening with rain and quite cold. Your four heroines decided to stay home and have their dinner at the Grosvenor hotel. After that Suzy and Magna retired to their rooms. They both requested a fire for the fireplace, which was set up at an additional 500 Rupees each. This was money well spent, turning the cold room into a cozy place when one sat by the fire.

Suzy opened a bottle of wine, read in her book and stared into the fire. When all the wood was exhausted, she went to bed. Khun Amorn only came back to the room well after midnight. He had had a hot night with one of the waiters in one of the neighbouring (cold) rooms.

It must have been the nose and youth factor. He was so fascinated by the huge and sexy nose of that 18-year-old waiter. That naïve Sri Lankan boy had bought that Amorn was only 25 years old. Khun Amorn was a bit embarrassed when he heard that the mother of his catch was only 40 and therefore belonged to his own age group. And he committed a real crime when he did not report to Suzy Size that Mr. Samantha had knocked at their door when she was having a shower.

With his flat nose and dark skin he was not Khun Amorn's type. But your heroine would have loved to share her wine — and other things — with that divine driver.

HAPPY HIKKADUWA DAYS
Another heart broken in Galle

The most scenic drive of the whole trip was from Nuwara Eliya down to the coastal town of Hikkaduwa. From an altitude of almost 1,900 metres you come down to sea level, passing uncountable green tea plantations, waterfalls, hills and mountains.

Had Suzy and Magna Size come without their somewhat snobbish Thai boyfriends, they would probably have taken one of the trains down. But since there was only second or third class available, this was no option for the spoilt Thai queens.

Your four heroines stopped at Devon Falls and had delicious tea and yet another one of those famous chocolate cakes. Mr. Samantha drove through the hills and the winding roads, but when he arrived in Hikkaduwa, he passed the town centre and continued in direction of Galle.

When Suzy complained, the reason became clear: he had a 'friend' with a hotel somewhere in the middle of nowhere and wanted to get a hefty commission. But all four travellers wanted to be within walking distance of town. Mr. Samantha finally turned around and drove back.

The first hotel they tried was completely empty and rather pricey, but the owner, a Sri Lankan woman, would not offer any discount. They tried next door at Sunil Beach Hotel, where they got rooms for US$30, including a hearty breakfast. And Mr. Samantha received a commission here too, plus a nice tip on top.

They spent a few happy and lazy days in Hikkaduwa, which is a bit run-down due to a lack of tourists and therefore money. When Magna left the premises of the hotel to explore the beach on first morning, she was immediately approached by a surfer who offered to take her to a 'quiet place'. There must be good reasons for the very visible sign at Sunil Beach Hotel that prohibits any guests from having visitors.

But it is actually not necessary to take in strangers. The Thai tourists were friendly with all the male employees of appropriate age and Khun Amorn in particular made many catches. One of the barmen openly showed an interest in Magna and Suzy, and confided not to like girls at all, but he was not either of the sisters' type.

Suzy fondly remembers her first few visits to Sri Lanka many years ago. Back then, your still-youthful heroine could not pass any construction site without seeing workers offering a blowjob by using their tongues to mimic rather obscene, but very agreeable acts with their mouths. Bisexuality must have been rampant in this country for centuries.

Think of Ebbe Kornerup. This gay Danish writer travelled through Thailand in the 1920s and wrote a book titled *Friendly Siam*, which reads like a historic Gay Guide between the lines.

But did you know that the same guy also wrote a book about Sri Lanka, which was formerly called Ceylon? Also remember Arthur C. Clarke, the gay science fiction writer, who made Sri Lanka his home for many, many years.

The British masters in Colonial times must have been appalled by the unmanly conduct of their subjects and introduced those silly and sinister sodomy laws, which are still in place today despite the obvious gay or bisexual reality.

One day your four heroines went on a little excursion. They rented two *tuk tuks* for 2,000 Rupees each (about US$20) and drove to the famous Unawatuna beach. It is still a very pretty beach for a swim or a stroll. Many people died here during the devastating tsunami in 2004, but all the buildings have been rebuilt, many in exactly the same, dangerous spots.

When Suzy first visited Unawatuna beach about 25 years ago, she was always invited by some young man to go to a 'quiet place'. But this time around, the four of them only stayed here for a short time for a snack; not that short time that you might have expected, gay tourist to Sri Lanka.

On the way to the old Galle Fort, they watched some fishermen reeling in the catch of the day. A very long net is placed far out at sea with a boat and then pulled in by two groups of men at both ends. It is hard work and can take hours. One third of the catch goes to the owner of the net and the other two thirds is divided among the workers. But on this day there were only a few very small fish caught and the meals at the fishermen's houses were probably very meagre.

In Galle, they walked around in the old town that was built by the Dutch. Of course, Suzy wanted to have a look at the Galle Fort Hotel where your heroine stayed in 25 years ago. Back then, birds flew freely in and out of the rooms and the guests used mosquito nets at night. The rooms were inexpensive then, but that is not so nowadays.

A gay couple took over the hotel ownership some years back and they have lovingly restored it to its former glory, as well as added an expensive fusion restaurant, and have thus turned the hotel into something far above your poor heroine's budget.

Colonialism was partly supposed to spread the word of the Lord and convert heathens into Christians, into true believers. The Dutch built their pretty Reformed Church in Galle between 1752 and 1755 and the 188 members "had their own church-chairs, carried by their slaves". You have not seen Galle, if you do not stroll around the old fortification that withstood the tsunami.

Our Thai friends did not walk very much due to the terrible sun that turns beautiful white or fair skin into deep brown or even black skin. How horrible! They even borrowed the umbrella Suzy Size had found about two years ago in a Zurich commuter train.

Suzy has carried this umbrella all around the world in rain and shine and it proved to be effective against the merciless sun in Galle too, especially if you take additional shelter in the shadow of a wall.

But Suzy and Magna endured the sun heroically and walked around the old fortification which proved to be very cruisy indeed. When the two sisters met a young man in one of the corners behind a wall that provided some privacy, Suzy had a hunch and left Magna alone with that tall guy. Magna remained in the company of that fellow for quite a while and later confided that it took less than a minute to get that cock out of those pants.

Your heroine would also have had her chance. She was approached in Galle Fort by a man who invited her into his house and most probably into his life. When Suzy showed no interest due to the not-so-tender age of said fellow, he offered to come along to Hikkaduwa. The friendly offer was made and refused several times.

And that is how Suzy Size broke another heart in Galle Fort!

DICKMAN RESORT: THE MAGIC PLACE IN NEGOMBO
But Gomez Place is an inexpensive alternative

When driving along the slightly shoddy dirt road that leads from Negombo beach (Poruthota Road) to the entrance of the somewhat secluded Dickman Resort, Khun Amorn once more doubted the wits of Suzy Size.

"Where the hell are you bringing us now?" The question was written all over his panic-stricken face. "My God, is this really the right way?" he asked and remained more than skeptical when Suzy just nodded.

After all, your heroine knew better, she had been here before and had always wanted to return. And as soon as they entered the gate of Dickman Resort, Khun Amorn, too, changed his mind.

It was the architecture (influenced by great Sri Lankan architect Geoffrey Bawa), the bold, unusual colors, the light, the height, the blend of water and nature, the salt water pool with a magic eye on the wall, the mirror in the door that suggests there is another pool behind the wall... all these elements combined have a great impact on any visitor.

Khun Amorn was a bit angry with Suzy. "Why did you not tell me?"

For good reasons, my dear. He was going back to Thailand with Khun Sun that very night, and was not to derail the not-too-secret intentions of your heroine.

Magna Size, Suzy's older sister, was also impressed by the stylish resort. All four were offered a welcome drink containing arrack and passion fruit juice, among other tasty ingredients, by the friendly Dutch owner — yes, his name is really Mr. Dick.

Suzy had only known him via emails up till now and was glad to finally meet him in person.

Returning to Dickman Resort was like coming home. They gave Suzy the same Purple Room as last year and your heroine had charming Chaminde, the able manager, explain again and again how to use the room's safe.

Well, gay tourist to Sri Lanka, a stay at Dickman is not cheap, but it is certainly worth it. There are only eight rooms available and the whole experience is unique. Magna did not stay at Dickman after all and moved over to inexpensive Gomez Place, just across the street. And thus your two heroines are able to give you some insight on both Negombo hotels that are suitable for the discerning gay traveller to Sri Lanka.

The four friends had a last dinner together at Bijou Swiss restaurant, just walking distance away. The fresh seafood that the two Thais ordered and your heroine's lobster thermidor (roughly US$20) was delicious.

After dinner the Thai boys went for a walk, but it soon became quite a long one. Suzy was a bit worried. If they missed the plane that night, they would be forced to stay on for another four days and that was definitely not intended.

When Suzy and Magna got bored waiting for them to return and left for a drink at Lords, they asked the waiters to tell the boys of their whereabouts, if they should return. But those worries were unfounded as Suzy and Magna bumped into their boyfriends just a little while later, to find that they had already introduced themselves to two quite obviously gay young men. They exchanged mobile phone numbers and then followed Suzy and Magna to Lords for a last drink.

Later that night, the two Thais took a taxi to the airport and returned to the land of the free. Finally, freedom for Suzy Size! Naturally, your heroine took advantage of it that very first night.

Look, gay tourist to Sri Lanka, you have to be able to read between the lines if you want to understand what does, can or might happen at Dickman Resort.

You will probably start the day with a delicious breakfast at the little restaurant. Suzy was checking her mails and the international newspaper with the high-speed wifi while eating her fried egg and drinking that delicious Sri Lankan tea. Chaminde or another one of the boys would join your heroine for a little morning chat and host Mr. Dick would do the same.

Then Suzy might go for a walk around town or Negombo beach and meet — by pure coincidence — a friendly young man on the way back or wherever. Suzy might have taken him to her room to show him her priceless stamp collection. But he might have turned out to be little interested in stamps and the many different ways that they can be collected.

Later on, Suzy learned that he had been banned from Dickman Resort and your heroine thereafter had relaxing massages only with Dickman staff or walk-in masseurs who were not banned.

Another way to enjoy oneself would be to lie down near the pool on one of the desk chairs. Once in a while a swim in the pool may seem appropriate, an undertaking not too stressful for those in the age group of your greying heroine.

Every day, a kingfisher would join the guests of Dickman and take several dives into the pool. All the guests talked about that special bird. One might suspect perfect host Mr. Dick had trained it to do that trick, but such suspicion is unfounded, the bird could obviously feel the peaceful and magical atmosphere at this unique resort and surely performed without bribe.

There might also be a walk-in pool player bending deep over the table with his cue. Was he really smiling at Suzy Size, or was your heroine suffering from illusions again?

A chat may follow; those Sri Lankan men can all speak some

English at least. If another guest was quicker than your sometimes slow heroine, the Dickman staff could get the number of said pool player and arrangements could be made for another good time later on. If in desperate need of one of those massages, most employees of Dickman could give one at almost any time and it would be interesting to test the waters. How far can one go? A playful pastime, indeed.

It may happen that Mr. Dick will offer you a glass of Champagne as a sundowner. And while you tell him about your life in half an hour, he might tell you his over another half hour. And before long your heroine and the Dutch gentleman might have emptied the whole bottle; time just flies at Dickman Resort.

Suzy might have another massage before going over to Gomez Place to meet Magna for dinner.

Gomez Place is not as stylish as Dickman, but still a very nice alternative since the room rates are about a third in comparison. There is also a small pool here and all the rooms come with the usual amenities, some even with a kitchenette.

And, yes, gay tourist to Sri Lanka, there are also many young walk-in men to be met here. Gomez is a nice guy, a caring host that looks after his guests well. Magna Size liked it so much, she is now considering fleeing the Songkran madness and hiding at Gomez Place, which is located in a Catholic neighbourhood and therefore should be free of the water craze that normally takes place in Thailand during the Buddhist New Year.

Magna and Suzy Size had dinner three times at Lords, a gallery, cocktail bar and fusion restaurant within walking distance from their hotels. It is owned and managed by Martin, an Englishman born in 1967. To watch Martin run his operation is worth a visit alone.

Even though he has very good-looking male staff, he seems to run around all night, taking orders and delivering them himself, even writing the bills. But despite his obvious stress, he is always friendly and attentive towards his guests. And his food is inexpensive and delicious. Suzy Size liked that place very much and will always return when in Negombo.

A NIGHT IN BANGKOK STILL MAKES A HARD MAN STUMBLE
Thailand

13

THOSE WERE THE DAYS, MY FRIEND

Your old heroine can still be spontaneous. One Saturday morning, she called the Malaysia hotel in Bangkok and made a reservation for that very night. The occupation rates of hotels all over Thailand are not very high these days; one even can get a room at the normally well-booked Malaysia at short notice for a dirty weekend.

Suzy Size grabbed her tooth brush, a shaver, some condoms, a shirt and one underwear and off she went. Even though Miss Size is a lousy driver, the trip to Bangkok from her Castelgandolfo residence is easy and does not usually take more than two hours. As the traffic was really light, Suzy pulled up in front of the Malaysia in no time.

The Superior room at this conveniently-located hotel is still only 808 Baht (about US$25), a bargain. The staff remembers Suzy, who has visited that unique hotel for many, many years. They are extremely friendly. The rooms at the 30-plus-year-old hotel are basic, but have everything you need: air conditioning, a fridge, a bathroom with two towels (even if you book a single room) and a TV set with international channels. And last but not least, there is a bed, too. Actually, your heroine's room had one queen size bed and a smaller one — even a threesome would have been possible without squeezing. But, anyway, such considerations were for later, for now Suzy wanted to do her day programme.

At Chatuchak, the famous Bangkok weekend market, Suzy could

not help but notice the sign that asked Thais to start loving Thais again, instead of killing each other: "Together we can."

But it is doubtful that such signs (you see them all over town these days) will do anything to restore the social fabric of this deeply divided country. Red shirts. Yellow shirts. Suzy prefers no shirt.

Your heroine walked from Chatuchak to the Saphan Khwai Skytrain station. Years ago there was an extraordinarily beautiful amulet seller in this area whom Suzy deeply admired. Every time your heroine was nearby, she would come and stare at him. She had talked with him a little bit about those silly amulets, and even stole a picture of him once. But alas, he is now gone and so has the beauty of the place.

Suzy travelled by Skytrain to Siam Square and then walked to Central World, or whatever is left of it after the Red Shirt protesters burnt it down, before they were driven out by the army. It is a sad, even devastating picture. The volcano has erupted. But for now there is calm.

Many Thais and tourists take pictures of that gigantic former shopping centre. The Thai Chinese family owners have said they will rebuild it as soon as possible, but it will certainly take a while.

Suzy had some sushi at Zen, the Japanese restaurant in Soi Convent, and then returned to the Malaysia hotel for a shower and a nap. Of course she checked the Coffee Shop first, but there was no local talent there at the time and your heroine stayed alone for now while she napped and prepared for a long Bangkok night.

In the old days, twenty or maybe even ten years ago, Suzy Size would have started the evening or a dirty weekend at Babylon sauna, just around the corner from the Malaysia hotel. Huge Babylon, with all the amenities you can think of, is certainly the best gay sauna in Asia, perhaps even in the world.

Initially, the Thai potato queens would come here to meet the Farang rice queens, which worked very well for both sides. Even the oldest and ugliest Farang would get laid here as many times as he could perform, with no money involved.

With the emergence of the gay tourists from Asia — mainly Hong Kong and Singapore — the mix has changed. There are more Asian rice queens here nowadays that compete with the Farang rice queens, but Babylon is still the gay heaven for everybody and if you cannot get laid here, perhaps seriously consider suicide.

The next stopover of such a typical and traditional Bangkok gay night would take place at Telephone Bar in Silom Soi 4. All the tables had working phones and one could call a prince charming or could be contacted by an interested local guy that might become one's companion for the night.

After some drinks and lots of talk at Telephone, the crowd would normally split up. Half would go to Soi Pratoochai more or less opposite the Surawong hotel, the other half to DJ Station in Silom Soi 2, the most famous gay disco of Bangkok.

In Soi Pratoochai are the commercial bars, with money boys wearing a number tag. Here they have the boldest gay sex shows in town. Gone is sleazy Twilight, and so is the *gothoi* (ladyboy) owner who used to sell overpriced beer by the glass and thus ripping off her customers. There are still Dreamboy and Bangkok's Best Boys (amongst others), where they have fucking shows when the police are looking the other way.

The Bangkok police look the other way most of the time. Suzy Size once hired a whole trio after the show to perform for her in private at the short time rooms of the Surawong hotel.

Those were the days (or the Bangkok nights), my friend, we thought they would never end, but which often ended at the infamous 24-hour coffee shop of the Surawong hotel where desperate souls could still make a last catch. Nowadays, your nearly frail heroine cannot do the full Bangkok gay nightlife programme any longer, she — realistically — has to cut back a bit.

Around 10pm, Suzy Size went from the Malaysia to Silom Soi 4 to have some beers at Balcony just opposite Telephone, which is her headquarters nowadays when in Bangkok. An old Swiss friend joined her and the two ladies chatted happily. Contrary to the sad state of Central World, Soi 4 was full of life, filled with lots of drinking revellers. There was no sign of crisis. Everybody seemed happy to be back. Later on, Suzy even went to the noisy DJ Station, which was completely full. The crowd was so huge, your heroine soon felt quite claustrophobic and left without an old or new friend in tow.

But that is the advantage when you stay at the Malaysia: the infamous Coffee Shop is open 24 hours, all night long, and many young men — and some policemen, too — come here to drink the night away. Suzy was soon joined by an attractive local talent who was eager to do a so-called massage.

The next morning, Suzy felt a lot like the burnt down Central World. Must have been that great sex. Or the many Chang beers. Or both.

A night in Bangkok still makes a hard man stumble.

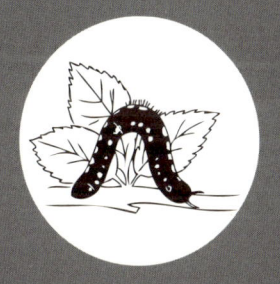

BATTLES
Thailand

14

BATTLES WITH BUTTERFLIES
An unfaithful gardener flees the scene

Not much to complain about, but not much is happening either. Suzy Size is a bit bored these days. The Pattaya routine has your heroine in its tight grip.

Saturday is still the highlight, it is beach day. But last week it started raining shortly after her return. And the *Mia Noi* was in Bangkok. No sex then, there was no one else in sight right in Jomtien in the rain. Does it matter? Not really. Next Saturday is another day for the Pattaya routine.

It rains a lot lately. The mushrooms are mushrooming in the garden. When the new gardener, Khun Aeh, has cut all the grass, he can start right over again. It is a Sisyphus task, somewhat depressing.

Why not go on another trip? Good old Suzy is a bit tired of travelling at the moment. And there is another pet project of your heroine: her Graviola tree plantation.

And on this front she wants to see some progress before sailing to new and foreign shores. And boy, it is really not easy!

When Suzy Size was on her last trip, Khun Amorn fired the gardener, Khun Mon. He then hired his brother, who moved into Castelgandolfo from Nong Khai. This is the typical Thai clan politics or corruption.

But not after long the brother returned to Nong Khai; his wife could not handle the hard work of rice cultivation alone. Suzy at least had her guest room back, but no gardener to do the heavy stuff.

Your heroine is a diligent girl, but just lacks the physical strength for certain tasks in the garden. She pressured Khun Amorn to find a replacement quickly. He was slow and uninterested as usual, but Suzy got on his nerves by nagging constantly. Finally, he brought one in from Kalasin; he was the young cousin of Magna Size's gardener.

And Khun Aeh worked well. Well, on the second day Suzy found him in the garden at around 10.30am, sound asleep. But after Khun Amorn woke him up, he did a fine job. And he was supposedly not feeling well that Monday morning. Could be true, but could have been a weekend hangover as well.

While Khun Aeh cut the grass and weeded the lawn, Suzy could achieve at least some things: she has now placed exactly 2,000 potted Graviola trees in groups of 100 in the garden. It is a tree almost unknown in Thailand, which bears large and tasty fruits.

The little trees grow much slower if they are exposed directly to the sun, so Suzy put the newest ones into places that provide half shade, they seem to like that. There are another 700 or so potted Graviolas under the black plastic mats of the green house that filter out up to 90% of the sunlight. They should remain there for another two months. And there are another 2,000 seedlings ready to be potted in those practical concrete rings.

Suzy Size is well on track to reach her goal of producing 2,500 Graviola trees a year, selling them, becoming filthy rich and thus being able to travel for forever and a day. But there are setbacks, of course. Your heroine is battling with caterpillars every day.

As soon as the sun is out, even during the shortest intervals of rain, these horrible butterflies swarm around the precious Graviola trees and lay their dreadful eggs. They always lay them on the newest and therefore most tender leaves. The caterpillars develop in no time, eat large amounts of leaves, and grow quickly to enormous sizes. They will strip the whole small tree of all of its leaves, if Suzy does not interfere.

But your heroine is alert. Not only does she destroy the eggs if she spots them, she kills the caterpillars with one elegant step of her high heel. This is her caterpillar tango.

Khun Aeh was diligent at first, but then he fell sick. On Thursday, which was the first day of the month, he did not show up for work. On Friday, the same, he probably had food poisoning, since he was shitting and vomiting at the same time, all alone in his unfurnished lousy little room for 1,300 Baht a month.

He was not fit on Saturday as well. But everything seemed well on Sunday. His cousin, Magna Size's gardener, had seen him and he was well. But on Monday he did not show for work again.

When Khun Amorn was finally able to reach him, he was already back in Isarn. He had taken his salary for the first two weeks from Suzy on Wednesday and fled the scene without a word.

Actually, Suzy can understand him to a certain extent. He had left home for the very first time. He had to face working hard, and being housed miserably, in a room without even a bed. He would have been paid 8,000 Baht a month, which is relatively generous, but would you want to work so hard for that amount?

What Suzy still cannot understand is the way of leaving without a word, for fear of loss of face. It is so typically Thai. But, Khun Amorn had lost face as well...

After his severe loss of face, Khun Amorn — who was responsible for the whole mess by first firing the old gardener and secondly hiring his brother, and then now the unsteady one — graciously agreed, no, even suggested taking Khun Mon back, the guy he had fired.

Khun Amorn knew very well that Suzy would otherwise not stop nagging and blaming him. Khun Mon started yesterday and there is hope that Suzy Size will reach her great gardening goals quite soon...

Today is another Saturday. The *Mia Noi* is back from Bangkok, the sun is shining. Jomtien beach is waiting.

ABOUT THE AUTHOR

Swiss-born author Hans Fritschi studied German and English Literature at university and worked for seven years as a journalist with a Zurich daily. In 1991 he relocated to Thailand where he became a freelance journalist and editor. He was also co-owner of a small publishing house and founded several magazines, including Thailand's first gay magazine. Since selling his business, he has travelled across Asia from his home outside Pattaya to explore the region's gay scene.